An
Irish Country
Childhood

An
Irish Country
Childhood

MARRIE WALSH

———◆———

A bygone age remembered

BLAKE

Published by Blake Publishing Ltd,
3, Bramber Court, 2 Bramber Road,
London W14 9PB, England

www.blake.co.uk

This edition published in hardback in 2004

ISBN 1857825861

British Library Cataloguing-in-Publication Data:

A catalogue record for this book is available from the British Library.

Design by www.envydesign.co.uk

Printed in Great Britain by CPD

1 3 5 7 9 10 8 6 4 2

Text copyright Marrie Walsh

Papers used by Blake Publishing are natural, recyclable products made
from wood grown in sustainable forests. The manufacturing processes conform
to the environmental regulations of the country of origin.

Every attempt has been made to contact the relevant copyright-holders,
but some were unobtainable. We would be grateful if the appropriate
people could contact us.

I dedicate this book to the memory of my late husband, Tom, for his encouragement and support while I was writing it, and also to the late Peter Barrington, my friend and mentor

CONTENTS

	PREFACE	ix
CHAPTER 1	HOME	1
	MAP OF MY VILLAGE	4
CHAPTER 2	OUR SCHOOL	11
CHAPTER 3	THE VISIT TO MY GRANDPARENTS	20
CHAPTER 4	GREAT-AUNT ELLEN	28
CHAPTER 5	SUNDAYS AND HOLY DAYS	40
CHAPTER 6	THE MISSION	46
CHAPTER 7	PAT AND MARY	50
CHAPTER 8	THE SISTERS	57
CHAPTER 9	DENNIS AND HIS MOUNTAIN DEW	62
CHAPTER 10	THE CAPTAIN	68
CHAPTER 11	THE BOGEY MAN	74
CHAPTER 12	THE HERMIT	77
CHAPTER 13	TOM AND SLIPPY	85
CHAPTER 14	KITTY AND LARRY	91
CHAPTER 15	THE TOFF	99
CHAPTER 16	GREAT-UNCLE HAMISH	106

CONTENTS

CHAPTER 17   THE BRIDEOGS   112

CHAPTER 18   LENT AND ST PATRICK'S DAY   116

CHAPTER 19   THE NEIGHBOURS   121

CHAPTER 20   THE THRESHING   128

CHAPTER 21   TOPSY AND POLLY   133

CHAPTER 22   TINKERS   139

CHAPTER 23   THE TRAMP   144

CHAPTER 24   COUSIN JOHN   148

CHAPTER 25   AEROPLANE   154

CHAPTER 26   MATCH-MAKING AND WATTLING   159

CHAPTER 27   THE WAKE   165

CHAPTER 28   THE O'FLYNNS   169

PREFACE

I WAS BORN in 1929, so the period I write about in this book is the 1930s and early 1940s. I left Ireland in October 1946. Our village is situated about seven miles from Ballina, a town on the River Moy near Killala Bay, County Mayo. In my youth our village was a thriving community of many families. People relied on each other as money was scarce and everyone had to work hard to survive. The land was poor and little of it was suitable for growing crops, surrounded as we were by bogs, hills and water. Luxury was a full stomach and being clothed. We had no modern conveniences and the ass and cart was the only mode of transport for many of us. Yet people were happy with their lot and a wonderful community spirit prevailed.

When I wrote this narrative in 1988, my village was a ghost village. Only two families still lived there, my own family home was unoccupied and most of the other houses were in ruins. On visits to Ireland for holidays I would revisit the scenes of my childhood. When I walked through the deserted village tears would stream down my face as I bade those kindly neighbours, long-since dead, a fond greeting. In my mind I would restore them to their rightful places and tell them who I was and that I had not forgotten them. Eventually I decided that I could not let the village die and started to write down my memories of childhood and especially of those wonderful people who so enriched my young life.

Now, in 1995, the village has happily been restored to life again as people from all over Europe vie with each other to purchase those ruins and convert them to their former glory. Children are again using the bog road to schools, and cars and jeeps have replaced the bicycle and the ass and cart. The farm-houses have all the modern conveniences and a personalized German post-box now stands at the end of the boreen.

If the spirits of the long-since dead revisit their old homes, I hope that they will not be envious of the new occupants' more relaxed lifestyle. In turn, I hope that the newcomers will be worthy trustees of homes and lands that were once wrested from the wilds by people whose harsh rulers forced them to survive in the wilderness. May all live together peacefully in the future and be as content as we were in my childhood.

CHAPTER 1

HOME

I N 1868, WHEN my grandfather decided to build his house of local stone and mortar with a roof of thatch, he first of all sent for the parish priest, as was the custom, to bless the site and advise on where the dwelling was to be constructed.

A site had already been chosen by the family on the opposite side of the road, which was then a pathway. The priest forbade my grandfather, Shaun, from building his home on this proposed site, giving no explanation, save to add that on no account was he ever to house either man, beast or fowl beyond the pathway. The priest then pointed out a suitable location and duly blessed the piece of ground and the chosen builders.

Then began the process of digging out the foundations, removing tons of earth and rock as the chosen site happened to be a hillock. However, when the house was finished, the surrounding ground levelled and stone walls built to shore up the loose soil, it fitted snugly into the remainder of the hillock, protected from the inclement weather and the chilling high winds which were prevalent in winter in our part of the country.

This house my mother eventually inherited with a few acres of land, and this was where I was born, the ninth child in a family of fourteen.

The windows were situated at the south side of the house, and looking out of any of them you were at eye level with a field which was called *Garrai Ban* or White Garden. Lifting the eyes to the distance, you beheld the hills known locally as *Cnoc-na-Suile* (Hill of the Eyes), as the two bumps gave the impression of two eyes peering down on the village. Standing at the front door and looking right, about half a mile as the crow flies, lay the Trassey Hills, where the gentle breezes flitted along the hillside, caressing the wild grass and heather, throwing up shadows that moved like waves on a seashore, and changing colour as they sailed along before being lost in the distance.

To the back of those hills stretched the majestic range of the Ox Mountains, like a nursemaid protecting her charges. The unusual colour of this quartz formation seemed to be navy blue, but the weather was constantly playing games, mixing the colours according to its mood.

This was the glorious sight I first saw from the safety of my mother's arms and which is imprinted on my memory. They were our roots, always there, always reliable, almost an extension of the family. As a child, I would sit on the stone wall as if hypnotised, imagining that the world ended where the mountains and the sky met and wishing I could stand at the top and touch the heavens.

In the opposite direction, away in the distance, could be seen *Nephin Beog* and *Nephin Mor* (Big and Small), or the *Bean* and the *Babog* (Woman and Child) as they were affectionately called. These acted as weather barometers, as the first snows were visible on the *Bean* days before they fell to the ground. When the clouds covered the top of the peak, then rain could be expected. There were streams and rivers galore for us to play and splash in, with plenty of lakes where otters and water hens abounded.

As we were a large family and were not the possessors of a big farm, it was essential to cultivate every bit of arable land possible. We were surrounded by acres of common land and *shroicks* or rough land, where heather and wild grass and rushes grew in abundance. Certain families had a share in this so-called no-man's-land with only a bog-hole or stream to mark its boundaries. So when cattle were put to graze on these strips of land, they had to be constantly watched to keep them confined to their own piece of grazing.

It was a monotonous chore for us children so it was up to ourselves to find a way of relieving the boredom. There were

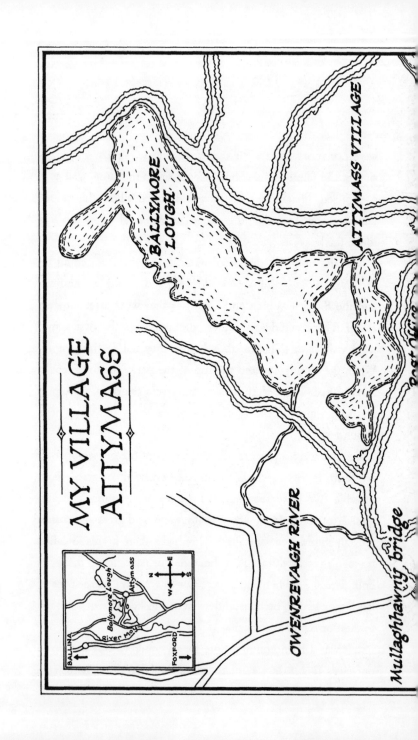

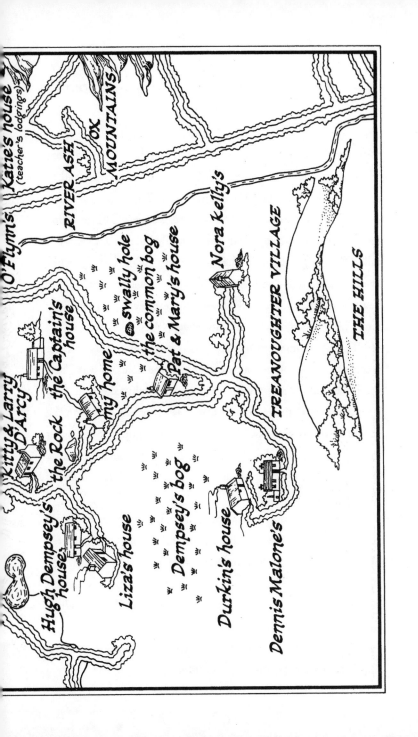

plenty of bog-holes to jump, and also flax holes. These were relics of bygone times, when flax was grown locally and had to be seasoned in deep holes in the marshes. They were now death traps, rumoured to be bottomless, and we were forever being warned against playing near these swally-holes, as they were called. We were also told that a monster called the alpluchor lived in those holes and that he was always waiting for man or beast to drop in so he could feast on their hearts, his favourite food. We listened, but we did not always obey.

The hot summer sun baked the crust that formed on the green, spongy, bubbling mass of fungi in the holes. It was like a witch's cauldron, and my brothers and I would take a running jump, landing in the middle of this crust. It would sink with the weight of our bodies, and up again it would pop, propelling us to the other side. We had found a perfect trampoline, and as we were out of sight of our homes, our parents were not aware of the danger we courted.

When the small rivers ran shallow in hot weather, we would build a *courigh*, or barrier, with stones and *clauber* – damp pieces of grassy earth from the river bank – to stay the flow of water. We would put lime into a sack, then secure the sack between the stones with the bag mouth opening into the flow of water. When the water volume built up, fish unwittingly became trapped in the bag. The lime stunned them and we would take the trout home to be fried in home-made butter.

HOME

The countryside offered us all kinds of delicacies: blackberries, bilberries, nuts, wild raspberries, sloes and haws. On a Sunday morning after early mass, men and youths would meet and go hunting across the moors and bogs, not for sport but for the pot. There were grouse, partridge, pheasant, rabbits and hares; also wild duck and geese, and woe betide anyone who killed out of season. There was a strict country code which, in latter years, as tourists came, was ignored. No longer would the pheasants' call be heard as they squabbled among themselves. Farmers eventually forbade all trespassing on their property in order to protect the wild life.

We would fish the rivers and lakes with home-made fishing rods and live bait. We would use heather to make besoms for sweeping the house floors and barns. Rushes would be used as bedding for the animals. At a certain time of year, when the hens were about to moult, we hastened this procedure by keeping them in darkness and feeding them on boiled nettles. We would then cut ling heather and carry great big bundles on our backs from the bogs. This would be used for bedding and the hens would gorge themselves, thus speeding up the process of growing new feathers.

We made use of most things that grew wild around our area, and learned from older people about country lore. A massive sycamore tree grew in the field above the house and one of my brothers would climb into its tall branches and put a rope over

7

the stoutest limb. We would then secure a piece of suitable wood to the ends of the rope and up and away we would go on the swing, into the air and over the rooftop of our house, back and forth, until our heads got dizzy, with everyone awaiting their turn and screaming in anticipation of the thrill of sailing over the chimneys. Mothers in the village would warn their children about accepting the challenge of a ride on our swing, but they still sneaked in for the forbidden treat.

Although our main source of heat was turf, sometimes we supplemented this by using logs. We never cut down trees indiscriminately, as they were essential as protectors against the elements. Sometimes an old neighbour would want a tree felled and would offer my father the wood on condition that he would cut the tree and take it away. He would get his cross-cut and saw and hatchet. He would put the hams and bridle on the horse and with several of us children in tow, carrying ropes and chains, we would set off.

First of all, we would tell the tree the reason for cutting it down. Then we would run around to the other trees and tell them not to cry. My father and brothers would mark the first cut with the hatchet, then rub soap on the cross-cut blade and start sawing. We would watch from a distance to see which way the tree would fall. As it creaked and crashed to the ground, the animals nearby would run in panic from the strange noise. The chains and rope would be secured to the tree and fastened to the horse's tacklings and off we would set on the homeward journey.

Some of us perched in the branches, swaying hither and thither as we tried to balance on this unusual conveyance. The road would be swept clean and all loose stones and pebbles dragged along against their will by this monstrous sweeper. Cattle would stop grazing and look in awe at the green giant, wondering if man had taken leave of his senses, as by this time we would have collected several children from houses along the way, all wanting a ride on our tree.

The tree would be deposited in a suitable place near the house and left all winter for the sap to dry out before it was fit for firewood. Some of it would be used as stakes for fencing. Then the fun would really begin. After school, and when all our chores were done, we would practically live in the tree. We climbed its branches, playing hide and seek and tig. We would tie a rope around the topmost strongest branch, pull it to the ground, then try to entice or dare someone to consent to be catapulted upwards. As we released the rope, the branch would leap back to its rightful position like a shot from a gun, sending this by now terrified creature, by nature earthbound, into kingdom come. But the thrill exceeded the fear and we all savoured the delight of going into orbit around our farm. No bones were ever broken, but we would be black and blue all over.

Months later, when the tree had seasoned, it would be chopped for various uses. If the trunk was a certain circumference, my father would make a creepy (a stool), which, when planed and smoothed and a cushion placed on top, made a very comfortable seat. Finally, when the once noble tree was denuded of all its vesture, we would gather all the debris, especially the *cipíns* or small sticks, and we would be allowed to make a fire in the old, disused lime-kiln, although it was a little worse for wear and overgrown with briars and weeds. We would spring-clean it and light our fire and once again the old kiln would come alive to the crackling noise of the sticks burning brightly, fanned by the mountain breezes, the scent of smoke reaching into its old heart, sending the warmth through its old stones and chasing the field mice. At last, the fire would die out and we would be called for bed, weary but happy.

CHAPTER 2

OUR SCHOOL

O UR NATIONAL SCHOOL was an impressive-looking building high above the road, with iron gates and wide steps each side of the dividing wall leading into the playground: boys to the left, girls to the right. In my schooldays, we were severely reprimanded if *Bearla* – English – was heard spoken in the playground, but when the school was built in 1879, our oppressors' laws forbade the teaching of our native language. However, children learned to speak Irish in their homes although they were unable to write it. The school was sheltered by the church, which blocked the view of the hills lying immediately to the east side and against which the church nestled.

Through the west windows could be seen the priest's house, a two-storey building with several entrances. To us it looked like a mansion with its carefully landscaped gardens and orchard,

1 1

the white, iron gates opening on to a wide drive which led to the hall door. The reverend father was a youngish man, sharp-featured, tall and lean. He always wore a black trilby hat. He rarely smiled and was not as highly respected as his predecessor. He could not communicate on a personal level with his parishioners and people thought he was unapproachable, so did not bother him except in dire need. From our classroom we would watch him read his breviary at the same time every day, slowly pacing from the hall door to the iron gates and back. At intervals he would partake of some substance from a small flask which he took from an inside pocket. In my innocence I thought then that it was holy water, but years later I realized it was good old Jamiesons. The house was always under surveillance with several pairs of eyes focused on its door. Nothing ever went unnoticed.

Our school was not big enough for the number of scholars it contained so we had to take it in turns with lessons. We would spend one hour sitting doing written work and one hour standing reading or around the blackboard or the hanging maps, which always intrigued us. We would pull the maps down to the utmost then let them snap back at breakneck speed. The cord would be lost and it would take the teacher hours to dismantle the map and put it right, while our knuckles smarted from the cane.

When the priest decided to pay us a visit, our teachers were promptly informed by the spies – the taller children who could see through the window facing the priest's house and kept watch for his appearance – so that everything was in order on his arrival. He would ask questions and many times would pull down one of the wall maps, get the pointer and we would have an impromptu geography lesson. We would be shivering in our skins in case we gave the wrong answer. The cane was often used after his departure if our performance was not up to the teacher's required standards.

The priest was also the school manager and selected the teachers, usually from his own part of the country as parishes seldom got a local pastor. He also dispatched them if they were not of the right calibre.

Bridget, the priest's housekeeper, was a kindly woman of middle age with a weight problem and an impediment in her walk. Her only excursions into the outside world were Sunday mass and an odd trip to town, when she was chaperoned by the hired hand. She suffered from sore eyes due to the constant smoke billowing down from the chimney, as her only means of cooking was the open hearth. The story goes that when the house was under construction at the beginning of the century, the lady who looked after the needs of the then parish priest refused the builders a cup of tea so they had their revenge by making sure that the chimney never functioned properly. Many times I heard Bridget call 'Bad cess' to her predecessor for her meanness in not being more liberal with her teapot.

A brook flowed through the grounds of the priest's house into the river close by and then into the lake. From this brook water was drawn every day to swill the old wooden-box toilets at the back of the school. This was done in chain-gang style.

Each morning there was an inspection of scholars. To the unfortunate child who had to be sent to the brook with carbolic soap and a scrubbing brush it was the greatest humiliation. Added to this was a further punishment when the parents heard the woeful tale through the usual channels of gossip.

The rule of the girls' school was hair length just to ear level, supposedly for hygienic reasons. How I envied the few girls whose mothers ignored the rule. As soon as they were outside the school gates they would loosen their plaits and let their flowing tresses blow free in the wind knowing they were admired by all their shorn friends.

The turf fires had to be lit by the older children, who took turns in coming extra early to school so the fires would be kindled when the teachers arrived. Each family had to donate a cartload of turf to both boys' and girls' school. On delivery, a class would be delegated the task of bringing the turf from the road to the shed. It was a welcome break from the daily routine. A teacher would supervise and would also comment on the quality of the turf and inform the donor's children, much to their embarrassment, if the standard was not up to requirements.

In summer time we were allowed to play outside the school grounds and our favourite pastime was jumping the river. Accidents often occurred and it was not unusual to see children huddled around the fire in the afternoon while their clothes dried. One fire was kept burning even in summer time with the kettle constantly on boil for the teacher's tea. We also picked the fruits that grew in abundance everywhere, and the teachers were forever warning us against eating unripened sloes as they had to cope with the results: violent stomach ache and sickness. To add insult to injury, we would afterwards get the cane for our disobedience. There was a natural sliding-stone on the hill behind the church. It was worn smooth by children over the years and we used to get walloped for wearing out our undergarments on it.

Our master and his wife and children drove to school in their pony and trap. One of the older children would be given the task of unharnessing the pony and putting him to graze in the local field, usually belonging to the parish. That same boy would get the pony and trap ready for the teacher's departure when school was over. The two other female teachers lodged Monday to Friday next door to the school at Katie's house. Katie was a widow with a son and depended on her income from the teachers for survival.

Katie was a good friend of Bridget, the priest's housekeeper, who used to cook the meat for the teachers' dinners. After school, I would collect the food from Bridget for Katie, as she was unable to negotiate the stile leading from the priest's house. The gates were only used by his reverence and as they creaked and groaned when opened they would have betrayed my presence. So I was warned to be swift and use the stile in case the priest wondered what I was furtively conveying from his kitchen.

One day I was hurrying across the stile with an offering from Bridget, in anticipation of sharing a bowl of jelly which had been cooling all day on the outside windowsill of Katie's house. This treat was reserved for a few chosen schoolgirls and had to be earned by bringing spring water from the well at playtime and other chores. In my haste, I slipped off the stile and on to the gravel path, and the contents of the dish that I carried were flung far and wide. When I retrieved them, covered in gravel, they looked like baby hedgehogs. I washed them in the brook and was amazed and nauseated to see that they were odd-shaped bits of meat. I had never seen kidneys before and to me they looked exactly like what was thrown out of the pigsty window after the pigs were castrated. I could never look at the teachers afterwards without remembering what they had eaten, and my share of the jelly went untouched that evening. Instead, I went home with both mind and stomach in turmoil.

The teachers were not local people and they never mixed

socially. Teaching was a very prestigious job in those days and if one happened to meet them after school hours out for their usual walk, we would run for cover rather than talk to them.

In summer weather the journey to and from school was full of adventure. Sometimes there were obstacles to be overcome, like the horse who would be grazing peacefully until he spotted us, when he would gallop towards the fence, neighing and prancing, trying to get out. We knew that he was vicious and had to be muzzled by his owner when he drew the travelling shop around the villages on certain days. Our parents never seemed to realize how frightened we were, but maybe the danger was not so great as we imagined.

Most of the road was open bog road with no fence and in winter no shelter. It could be treacherous and an adult from our village had to meet all the children from school, especially when the wind blew down from the mountains and the rain lashed at us mercilessly. Then we would have to walk in single file, holding on to each other, otherwise we would have ended up in a bog-hole.

Although this bog road was a short-cut to church, school and shops, it was seldom used after dark as it was supposedly haunted by the ghost of a poor, wandering soul who had drowned in a bog-hole. The ghost carried a pitch-torch and many an unsuspecting traveller would see its light in the distance. Using the old paths and the stepping-stones across the river, they would gladly hurry to meet their fellow-traveller. At a certain point, where the road followed part of the old highway, they would find themselves escorted by the invisible phantom. Its pitch-torch would glow in the dark night, but only part of a man's hand would be visible holding it. Then the phantom light would disappear into the bog, leaving the now-terrified human being to continue his journey, wondering whether what he had seen was real or a fear-induced delusion caused by hearing so many ghostly stories from childhood.

In summer we would pick blackberries, sloes, bilberries and nuts as we walked. We would thread the bilberries through long blades of wild grass. They resembled necklaces and we would come in from school with our hands, faces and teeth stained blue-black from the fruits of the countryside. We were allowed to walk along the river when it ran shallow and would feast on the wild raspberries that grew on the banks. They would drop into the water and our ducks would devour them with relish.

In scorching hot weather, when the sun deprived the bogs of moisture, the skeletons of the trees of centuries past presented themselves. They stood like sentries with their jagged stumps bleached white and ghostly, as if trying to reveal the glory that was once theirs before they were indiscriminately burned down. Their roots resembled long, bony fingers reaching out to touch and console each other in remembrance of their majestic past. In the moonlight they looked like shrouded spectres rising from the bog, trying to convey their former greatness, when they covered the land and held in their arms the birds of the air and harboured the many wild animals which roamed without hindrance through the Ireland of old. In winter they would again disappear into their watery grave, to be lulled to sleep by the moaning winds that roved through the bogs as if searching for the trees where they once played hide-and-seek.

We were not encouraged to dilly-dally on our way from school as there was always plenty of work awaiting us, but we would prolong the journey until the pangs of hunger overcame us. We did not have the benefit of school dinners in those times: only a few slices of soda bread which never lasted until lunchtime anyway. We would race across the last few fields home and devour everything in sight. We never asked what was on the menu, as hunger is good sauce. We would then change from our school-clothes into our *giobals* – worn, raggy garments – and would help around the farm. Everyone had their share to do and oftentimes there was no time for homework. That had to wait for next morning, to be hurriedly done sitting on the school steps before the teachers arrived. In winter, before bed, we would be scrubbed clean in a big tub of warm water at the end of the kitchen, but in summer we washed in the river. Bed would be welcome, then all too soon morning would come and we would set off for school once more.

CHAPTER 3

THE
VISIT TO MY
GRANDPARENTS

T HE EXCITEMENT THAT preceded our visit to my grandparents was enormous. This visit would be the first
night of the full moon, and our parents would bring
the usual gifts: home-made butter carefully patterned and
wrapped in muslin; apple, blackberry or rhubarb tart, currant-
bread and any other delicacy we could afford. My father would
strap the melodion on his shoulders and we would set out across
the fields at dusk, eagerly looking forward to a night of excitement.

The distance was about four miles and we had to pass
through several villages, exchanging pleasantries with one and
all. We took the old familiar path on these excursions: across the
river, jumping from stepping stone to stepping stone with our
shoes in our hands and our hearts in our mouths, then down the
bog road until we came to the school. We children would then

gallop up the hill to where the little church snuggled into the hillside. We would push open the side gate near the great tombstones that marked the resting place of past shepherds of the faithful, who had earned their rest in this peaceful setting. We would hastily pay our respects to the Blessed Sacrament as our parents bowed their heads in fervent prayer. Then we would tiptoe around the church admiring the lovely stained-glass windows portraying all the familiar saints. We would read aloud to each other the names of the donors of these memorials, long since departed from our mortal world. After this little sojourn we would again continue our journey.

At this point we could follow a scenic road by the lake but we preferred the old, well-trodden path used for centuries by the locals. It wound its way along the foot of *Cnoc-na-Haltoir* (the Hill of the Altar), so named because in penal times (the period from 1695–1829 when the Penal Laws placed many harsh restrictions on the native Catholic population of Ireland) the practice of our religion was forbidden, so priests had to say mass in the open. This was usually in the hills, with the altar hidden from view, but with good vantage points for the sentries who were posted to sound the alarm. The flat stone that formed the altar was still there, a sacred reminder of the troubled past. Our teachers would take us into this hallowed place as part of our local history lesson and we would reverently kiss the ancient monument and pray for the souls of the departed.

My father used to tell us that a tunnel ran underneath the hill near the path where we were walking, and that the entrance was opposite the church, close to the sliding-stone which all the children in the vicinity had used for generations. The smell of the wild flowers that grew in abundance everywhere tickled our nostrils, and the wild ling heather each side of the path scratched our bare legs as we passed in single file through the rugged but beautiful landscape.

We would gather bunches of wild hyacinths to take to our grandparents and would sometimes scare our parents by pretending to be lost as we hid in the long ferns. The birds would flutter and complain about being disturbed from their nightly shelter. Hares would bound across our path and disappear and my mother would say, 'Did ye see the fairy riding on his back?' and as we wondered why we never saw the fairy she would say to my father, Jim, 'Our kids need glasses,' and the hills would ring with their laughter.

Now we were crossing the *mayren*, or perimeter fence, and leaving the protection of the hill behind. The open road seemed to stretch for miles into a barren wilderness with no house in sight. It was a rough, stony road and we always walked to the side as rivulets of water flowing down the hills made channels through it. They used to say in that locality that the asses had stone-bruises. Eventually we would come within view of my father's village and our hearts would be beating like drums as we raced ahead, eager to meet all our relatives. The village of Cullane, where my father was born, was close to the Ox Mountains. It seemed to me when I was young to be a desolate place with stones and rocks everywhere. My grandparents' house was on the edge of the bog and the family must have been the last people to arrive there in centuries past. My father once told me that in times gone by his ancestors had lost their land. He did not explain how, but many people were dispossessed during penal times. In order to find somewhere to live they had to flee into the hills and mountains, where they cleared the stones and rocks with their bare hands to make fields. To this day the area bears testimony to the perseverance of a sturdy people who survived in the face of adversity.

My grandfather, Tom, was born in Cullane in 1857. Eventually he inherited the little farm and married a local girl, Ann Durkin, who was born in 1868. They had nine children, six boys and three girls, five of the family emigrated to the USA at the beginning of the twentieth century and never returned. My youngest aunt stayed to care for her parents and eventually she and her family inherited the farm.

We would be greeted with '*Cead mile failtes go lear*' – 'A hundred thousand welcomes' in Irish – and be paraded by our proud parents for all to comment on our development. There would be good-natured discussions as to whom we resembled and the usual banter exchanged. Then the night's enjoyment would begin. My father would play the melodion and we would sing songs passed down from generations past.

We children would dance around the big kitchen with our young cousins, and the children next door would join in the fun. Stories would be told and the grown-ups would gossip. The tea would be made and there would always be a special treat for the visitors. The night would be enjoyed by all, old and young, and all too soon it would be home time. As we took our leave, tears would be shed and promises made for a return visit the next full moon.

After visiting our grandparents, our parents always took the long way home by road. My brothers and I would be exhausted and it would be around midnight and well past bedtime. It was also the hour when all the spooks and spirits who were earthbound returned to do their hauntings. We were weaned on such stories and our childish minds conjured up all sorts of unearthly encounters.

We had to pass the field of the Hanging Tree – a tree that witnessed the death throes of the holy priests hanged for saying mass or of young men whose only sin was to be patriots. The graveyard was further on and we would hasten our steps with our eyes shut tight, gripping our parents' hands, our rosaries in our pockets; our hearts beating like drums, hoping the dead would let us pass unmolested.

These obstacles safely negotiated, we relaxed a little and told each other of imaginary sightings. Now we were on the stretch of road overlooking the haunted lake. The water lay shimmering in the moonlight in its idyllic setting and seeming to cast a spell on us. Twin emotions of fear and fascination would grip us – it was a kind of ecstasy, enticing us to look into its soul, daring us to unfathom its dreaded secrets. Would we behold the apparition of the spirits of the dead monks once more unbound to row across their beloved lake; to hear the swish of the oars as they skimmed over its surface – the boat caressing the waters as it did long ago?

The story goes that the monks were returning from the opposite shore with the last boatload of stones to finish the church they were building on the peninsula. Their hearts must have been bursting with joy as they rowed across to their little thatched hut on the other side, chanting their psalms. But, alas, fate had ordained otherwise. The boat was overloaded and it sank into its watery grave with all hands lost. How could this enchanting stretch of water be involved in a tragedy that was to haunt people for centuries? It was told that on the anniversary of this tragic occurrence, the lake released from its depths those it had claimed so prematurely long ago. On this night also the woods and fields and stone fences would re-echo the lamentations of a people long departed mourning their beloved monks.

To the mortal who beheld this apparition, especially on its homeward journey, it was a dire warning of some calamity befalling them or their family, or a disaster in the area. To witness the outward journey was a good omen. As we children gazed in awe as this peaceful lough, perhaps setting its stage for the re-enactment of its gruesome play, we were half-longing and yet fearful of it unfolding before us.

The ruins of the uncompleted church could be seen in the distance, gaunt and mocking in the moonlight as if waiting for the ghostly spectres to invade its walls and resume the task left unfinished. This was a building that had been denied its soul; deprived of the voices of the people praying in their flowery language; deprived of the holy mass being offered within its wall. Never again would it resound to the happy voices of the monks as they lovingly worked on their church.

Locals told the story that a church site had been sanctioned near where our present church now stood – it would be in a more central position for most people. But a wealthy landowner wanted the church built near his home so as not to inconvenience his family with a long journey to mass. He promised financial help and free land to the monks and his offer was accepted, with tragic consequence.

We were now in sight of St Joseph's Church and felt relieved to be back at this sanctuary of the Lord. We blessed ourselves reverently and thanked Him for a safe journey. As we passed on our way towards the river, we crossed a footbridge and climbed the steps leading to the road which was bringing us nearer home.

THE VISIT TO MY GRANDPARENTS

It was comforting to see the lights of our village in the distance and hear the dogs barking. We would cross the fields home and our dog would come bounding towards us, jumping with delight, welcoming us back. It was lovely to be home.

CHAPTER 4

GREAT-AUNT ELLEN

MY GREAT-AUNT ELLEN lived alone in the village of Carrowkerribla, about three miles from where we lived. She was the spinster aunt of my mother, and an old lady by the time I was born. She was unable to cope with the everyday chores and had to have the company and help of us children most of the time. Those three miles that I, on my own or with a brother or sister, had to walk, were fraught with danger, or so we thought. First we had to get past Ted Lynch's mule. Then a mile further on there was Connor's bull, grazing peacefully until he spotted us, when he would half-raise his head, as if deciding if we were worth a scare. He would then charge, frothing from the mouth, his hoofs pounding the earth. We used to imagine that he would scale the fence but his massive bulk prevented his doing so. We would run for cover, thankful that we had escaped.

Then, further along the same road, there was an empty house where the men o' the road (tramps) took temporary refuge. We would tiptoe past, scared in case they might do us some harm. Now we were leaving the boreen behind and coming on to the main road into another village, with a lake on one side and Dodd's farm on the other. This farm stocked a bull and a stallion. We could hear the bellowing of the bull before we came in sight of the farm. If those animals happened to be grazing in the fields bordering the road our lives were again threatened. The bull was fettered but he still pawed the ground and made deep rumbling noises, letting us know that he would make short work of us if given the chance.

The stallion would stand and toss his proud head in the air, neighing and showing his teeth. Sometimes we would watch from a distance as his handler exercised him. This was done by giving him enough rope, tied to a bit in his mouth, to gallop around in a circle. Then he would be led into his stable and we would continue on our way.

These obstacles safely negotiated, we still had some unfriendly dogs to contend with, but at last the journey to my great-aunt's was completed. We would tell her of the difficulties we encountered, but she would laugh and say that the animals sensed our fear and that was why they seemed threatening.

Her house was the last one in the village. On a fair-sized farm with good, arable land, this comfortable house with its thatched roof, lay snuggled among trees. These protected it from the fierce winds that in winter blew across the bogs that stretched as far as the eye could see. The purple heather grew in abundance on every sod-ditch that surrounded the north side of this dwelling, blooming everywhere it could find a foothold. Wild grass and rushes, plus myriads of wild flowers, all found space to flourish here. White cotton tips looked like bits of cotton-wool stuck on reeds, and in between there were little pools of water. This presented a spectacle beautiful to behold and was an ideal habitat for all kinds of wildlife: duck, pheasant, partridge, grouse, hares and rabbits, foxes, badgers and weasels. I used to hide on top of the sod-ditches, concealed by the heather and watch nature at work.

At nesting time, the parent birds would be seen scuttling through the undergrowth so as not to betray their nesting site. I would sneak a look at the various nests with the different-coloured eggs, my hand over my mouth in case the mother bird should catch a whiff of my breath. We were told that if we breathed on the eggs or on the fledglings, the mother would abandon them and that the parent birds would fly over the bogs and moors wailing for their little ones and cursing the humans who had robbed them of their family.

I once found a wild duck's nest built on one of these sod-ditches which was several feet high. I informed my great-aunt of this and was scolded for telling lies. A wild duck always builds on the ground she said, so I took her to see this beautifully constructed nest with the down plucked from the breast of the mother bird covering the eggs to keep them warm while she foraged for food.

My great-aunt was amazed. She said she had never seen the like and wondered how the duck would get the little ones to water. But mother duck had craftily built near a pond and eventually there was the family of golden-coloured, fluffy ducklings bobbing on the water with their proud parents.

Another day I was walking past a field of potatoes, daydreaming as usual, when I heard a commotion in and among the stalks, followed by a screech of terror. It was a weasel which had stalked a rabbit and had pounced with deadly precision. Afterwards I found the body of the rabbit. The weasel only drinks the blood. His trade-mark is a clean-cut hole at the base of the neck, much like a bullet hole. Ellen said that the meat is contaminated afterwards and is poisonous to humans. In Ireland, people had a fear of weasels. In olden times it was supposed that witches took this form. This animal was considered spiteful and malignant so people kept their respectful distance.

My aunt told me a story about three men who were once widening a road in the area and had to rebuild the stone fences knocked down whilst doing so. They came across a weasel's nest with young ones in it. Being aware of the mystery and might surrounding these creatures and of the consequences of killing one, the men moved the nest further down the ditch. Mother weasel, missing the nest, thought her family had been destroyed. She sneaked into the house where the men's dinner was being prepared. There were three mugs of milk already poured and seemingly the weasel poisoned them. Going out and finding the nest safe and sound she returned as the men were about to take their places around the table. She jumped up, put her feet on each mug, and tipped the contents onto the table as the bewildered men looked on.

My aunt also said that the mother weasel will protect her young with the tenacity of a bear, and if she feels they are threatened will rally help. Then all the weasels will lie in wait and ambush man or beast. They had once attacked a young girl who used a certain path to and from school. She probably found nesting sites and, being curious, she must have had a peep passing by. The weasels thought it was a threat and lay in wait and attacked, biting her in the back of the neck with their long canine teeth. She was found dead in the field by her parents who went searching for her when she failed to return from school.

Even the owl and the hawk, who are natural enemies of the weasel, may become victims themselves. They swoop on the weasel and grab him with their talons to crush him to death. Sometimes the weasel manages to turn and strangle his enemy in mid-air and they will both fall to the ground. Where the weasel will finish his meal and for vengeance will eat the brains of his adversary.

My great-aunt's brother, James, was a bachelor and since his death our family had the use of the farm. We supplied Ellen with all her worldly needs and she also had her old-age pension. We would collect this from the local post office. She would tell us to buy sweets, plus whatever shopping she needed. She liked to smoke a pipe, so tobacco was on the list. The shopkeeper would ask who smoked the baccy, knowing full well that it was Ellen. We would be embarrassed as it was unusual in those days for a woman to smoke, except in private.

Ellen was getting feeble by this time and she used to sit by the turf fire on a three-legged stool smoking her clay-pipe, her *doodeen* as she called it. She would nod off and the pipe would fall from her hands on to the hearth, until there was eventually only a stump of stem left. She would still drag smoke out of this semblance of pipe, making smacking noises with her toothless gums as she puffed away to her heart's content. She was small and skinny with a *smig* – a pointed chin – and long grey hair. She wore a long black skirt and shawl and, hunched over the fire, she sometimes resembled a witch. Every chance we would get we would steal a puff out of her *doodeen* and she would grab her stick and aim for our shins, calling, 'Bad cess to ye for stealing my baccy.' But we were fleet-footed and were soon out of harm's way.

We had to be ever watchful of her in case she toppled into the fire. No amount of coaxing would entice her to lie on her bed for a nap. She considered going to bed in the daytime a sin. When she was in humour she was a great story-teller. We pestered her to teach us her old songs; songs from way back. She used to say they were as old as the Connemara Hills.

She was a fluent Irish speaker and would translate for us. She had a woman friend of her own age who used to visit. They would gossip in Irish so fast that we could not understand. Winnie was her friend's name and she was as tall as Ellen was small. She always wore laced-up boots with hand-knitted *baneen* (home-spun wool) knee-length stockings, layers of flannelette petticoats and black, long, wide skirts. Coming across the fields she looked like a giantess. Ellen was always referring to her as 'the mountainy woman'. She came originally from a village near the mountains many miles away. This was Ellen's way of telling us that Winnie was not a local although she had lived all her married life, maybe fifty years, on the neighbouring farm. People were very clannish then. You were considered different if you were not a local. It might take a lifetime to be accepted.

On summer days we would sit on the banks of the river that flowed by Ellen's land. We were warned not to go near the water, but it drew us like a magnet. There was a natural harbour in one of the fields where the animals watered and the fisher-men, fishing for salmon, always brought their boats in at this point. They would sit on the banks and have a picnic. We were always included in this treat as we often brought the fishermen water from our spring-well or milk for the tea. We would often be rewarded with a sixpence which, to us, was a fortune. We would sit for hours talking with these visitors from England with our feet dangling in the water.

We were not allowed to fish the river, even from our own land. It was the property of a Captain Berry who lived in the big house on the opposite side of the river about a mile downstream. A vast acreage of land, including woods, belonged to this landlord: lands that were taken from the original owners. They were not bought, neither were they given. A stretch of the river was also leased to him for the use of his visitors, who only fished for sport. A water-bailiff, named Paul, was employed by this big landowner, who had business interests in England and who spent most of his time there while a manager looked after his Irish interests.

Paul, the bailiff, was a worthy trustee of his master's woods and river. He kept an eagle eye out for trespassers and woe betide any poachers caught by him. He always carried a gun and would fill their breeches with buckshot as quick as look at them. He also used to swear like a trooper and we were told to give him a wide berth. But when he rowed the visitors up the river to fish or picnic by or off our land, we would talk to him, and often sat in the boat watching the fishermen with their big, modern fishing rods with those newfangled reels and the different bait they used out of tins.

This was all new to us. We fished the lakes and small rivers around our home with home-made rods and caught live bait to lure the fish. A live frog was great bait for pike. We could show these grown men a few tricks when it came to catching salmon, but we just sat and watched and listened. If our land was used for harbouring the boat, custom was that we were entitled to a salmon from each catch. This was taken home to my mother and the family used to greet the appearance of this fish with exclamations of 'Oh, no! Not fish again.' We got fed up with salmon fried, roasted, boiled and steamed. Often we left the fish to rot on the banks of the river rather than drag it the three miles home.

Ellen used to tell us of the people who lost their lives in this river, saying it had an appetite for youngsters. She remembered a tragedy years before when a boat-load of young men and women were rowing across after a dance. Someone threw an apple and everyone rushed to get it. The weight, suddenly shifting, toppled the boat and all were lost.

She also told us of the story of St Patrick who, with his followers, was supposed to have tried to cross from the opposite side to land somewhere near where my great-aunt now lived. The first time, a flood stopped them and so they waited for the water to subside. They made camp for people and animals. The second time the local people stopped him by throwing stones, so he was forced to turn back in mid-stream, but he cursed the stone-throwers and told them they would always be beaten in battle. When they heard this they relented and allowed him passage, all except five people. On seeing this the saint withdrew part of the curse and told them that in all the battles they would be beaten in, they would never lose more than five people.

There was an aura of serenity and peace around Ellen's dwelling and anyone who spent any time there always remarked on the balming effect they experienced, especially in the field nearest the river. It was as if the ground itself held on to the holiness left behind by this saintly man and shared it out afterwards to anyone lucky enough to walk the same grounds.

Although my great-aunt's house was isolated, it had not always been so. Her parents lived through the famine years and used to tell her about the families who lived in a little village beside the bog road which she would point out to us in the distance. She would tell us of the seven families who lived there, all bearers of the same name, 'Barratt'. Not one family survived that terrible famine. It was a terrible time, 'a gra', she would say, when people died from the *feargortugh*, eating grass like the cow. They did not understand that nature had provided the cow with four stomachs. Man's digestive system could not cope, and so the grass killed him. They lay where they fell with the sky as their shroud, with no-one to dig their graves, and without the Holy Rites of the church. 'May God rest their souls,' she would murmur. And we would chorus, 'Amen'.

She would also say that the pools and little expanses of water that were plentiful in our area were the tears of the destitute who had suffered starvation in a country where food and grain were being exported. She was full of information and we never tired of listening to her. She had a wealth of stories, songs, verses and riddles; and willing pupils in ourselves.

My eldest brother inherited the farm when he married at the age of twenty-four and Ellen was now quite happy with the young couple to look after her. When she took ill I was staying at the house, helping to look after the new baby who was so welcome in a house that had not witnessed a birth for nearly ninety years. I was now twelve years old and was going to school from here. By now I had the use of a bicycle. I was sleeping in a makeshift bed beside Ellen, and one night she called me to get her a drink. She said she was dying and began to tell me the names of her family long-since dead who had come to meet her. She was talking to them as if they were in the room.

Before I left for school she gave me her blessing and when I got back that evening my dearest great-aunt was dead. She was my greatest teacher and had an important influence on my young life. She taught me a love of my native language and all it stood for, encouraging me to translate it into English and enjoy both.

GREAT-AUNT ELLEN

The first translation I have never forgotten, although I was punished for solving the riddle and finding the hidden message therein. It was suggestive but at the time I did not realize that. The mere fact that I solved the mystery was enough for me: it was the first word in every sentence.

> *When stormy winds are passed and gone*
> *Shall quiet calm return.*
> *I often saw in ashes dust*
> *Lie hidden coals of fire*
> *With good attention mark your mind*
> *You will a secret question find*
> *Sweet is the secret; mark it well*
> *Heart for heart, so now farewell.*

My great-aunt went to the Hedgerow school, as did my maternal grandmother, Biddy, her sister. Hedgerow schools grew up during the period of the Penal Laws (1695–1829) when the native Catholic population was denied education. The teachers taught in the open air – Irish, Latin and English – and were usually paid in corn or turf. The payment at my great-aunt's school was two sods of turf or a sheaf of oats. The field where it was held is in the next village by the lake, known as Durkin's *Lisseens* (fairy fort).

CHAPTER 5

SUNDAYS AND HOLY DAYS

HEN I WAS a child Sunday was a day of rest. That was a law of the Church and was strictly adhered to. Our pastors were in full control and if the sanctity of the Sabbath was violated by some unfortunate, the offender's name soon got to the ears of the priest. The only time the law was relaxed was at harvest time. If the weather was inclement and the crops in danger of being lost, only then would permission be given from the pulpit for people to work to save the crops. Otherwise, these holy days were a respite from the daily toil for man and beast.

Of course, food had to be cooked and animals and fowls fed, but generally most of the heavy work was done on Saturday. First mass was 9 a.m. and that was usually for the younger parishioners. Most of the chores were done, especially the milking, before they got home. A good fire with coals raked out from its heart would be ready to accommodate the frying pan and soon the lovely rashers of home-cured bacon, cut from the sides of bacon hung from the rafters, would be sizzling merrily. Eggs would be fried, usually turned for quickness, with no time to cater for individual taste such as sunny-side up as there were too many mouths to be fed.

Onions would also be cooked for the strong-stomached, plus any leftovers from the day before, such as boiled sliced potatoes, cabbage and the nicest delicacy of all, swede fried in bacon fat. As my grandfather Shaun used to say 'That fairly tantalizes the taste buds.'

Breakfast over, it was time for the parents and older members of the household to go to the 11.30 mass. Younger children usually accompanied them and we would go across the fields, the near way. We would then meet up with other villagers as we reached the road and would continue our journey, men and women gossiping, children running and skipping along, maybe jumping the odd bog-hole, or running into the disused sandpit, which was full of foul-smelling water covered with thick green slime. In spring, the frogspawn covered the surface of the small pit. We would lie on our stomachs and grab handfuls of the beady-eyed, jelly-like creatures. We called this 'po-frogeney'. We would run screaming to our parents, showing off, pretending it was real jelly, but all we got was a cuff on the ear and the promise of a good walloping when we got home for dirtying

ourselves. We would then be made to wash in the river before
we got to the church.

More excitement awaited us crossing the footbridge over
the river. We dared each other as to who could walk the plank's
edge. If we slipped, we fell into the raging torrent that rushed
down from the mountain and as this was also our way to school,
we courted danger daily without thinking of the consequences,
as very few could swim.

Coming home from mass, my mother would dally, talking to
people at several houses along the way. I would play with their
children and by the time we got on our way, we would be the
only ones on the road. Dinner would be ready and waiting and
we would be ravenous.

In summer, we would go visiting or friends and relatives
from the low-lying villages would visit us so they could accompany us up into the hills. People would be leaning over their half
doors as we passed through the village and it would be a lazy
walk as we chatted with all and sundry. We would take the old
familiar paths, used by locals and villagers from the other side of
the hill. It was a short-cut for them to church, school, post office
and shop. In olden times, before roads existed, these same
paths were used by the weavers in our village to take their wares
to market – a two-day walk there and back. They would walk in
their bare feet to save their *throicheens* – shoes woven from
straw. On nearing their destination, they would then cover their

feet. These stories we heard as we walked in their footsteps and we felt that they were alive to us somewhere, in those lovely surroundings.

We would pass the field of the rabbits, *Pairc-na-Gcoinini*. It belonged to a family who had long since given it over to those nervous little twitching creatures with their white powder-puff tails. The field could be ill-spared, but as it was home to hundreds of rabbits, it was pock-marked with their burrows and they pounced on every blade of grass that dared show its head above the ground. We would peep over the stone ditches and the rabbits would scarper underground. We could not understand how we could never catch them unawares, as we did not know that nature had endowed them with an all-round vision. We always carried salt with us, as the grown-ups used to tell us that if we shook a grain of salt on their tails, they were ours, and we were gullible enough to believe them.

We would wind our way to the top of the hill, *Cnoc-na-Suile* (Hill of the Eyes). We would be exhausted tramping through the heather and wild grasses, but we would be well rewarded as the view was breathtaking. Standing on the summit, we could see far and wide. The lovely Lough Conn and many other lakes and rivers, as well as houses and farms and villages far into the distance, were pointed out to us. Our outing was a geography lesson. We were familiar with people's dwellings before we knew the people themselves. We would then roll helter-skelter down the hillside until we got tired, while the grown-ups gossiped. Our clothes and hair would be covered in bracken and bits of heather and we would come home dishevelled and hungry, keenly anticipating our Sunday tea. This always included a treat, such as homemade current-bread and fruit tarts, depending on the fruit in season, or home-made jams and jellies and custard. We were not allowed tea as we were told it stunted our growth. Instead jugs of drinking chocolate, made with milk, would be placed in the middle of the big scrubbed kitchen table and the grown-ups would have tea or coffee. A special treat for the visitors would be potato cake, baked on a griddle on the open hearth, then put in a big mixing bowl when cooked and lashings of melted homemade butter poured over it. It was a great delicacy and much appreciated by our visitors as our family were renowned for their potato bread.

Then we would get out of the way, as Sunday night was dance night. The dancers would either walk or cycle a distance of between six and twenty miles, depending on the music provided by the owner of the dance hall. We would have to get out of the way as the young women of the village would gather at our house to titivate themselves. The waving tongs would be much in evidence – heated on the red-hot coals and tested on brown paper before being applied to the hair, sometimes singeing it. We found the smell nauseating, but nevertheless I sometimes longed to be grown up and suffering the same fate.

Then there would be plucking and pencilling of eyebrows and the same powder puff and rouge rag would be shared by all.

Our parents were very liberal minded and allowed a lot of freedom to their partly grown-up brood. Not so other parents in the village, who were quite strict, especially where wearing make-up was concerned. Therefore our house was open house and the starting point for nightly excursions. Good-natured banter and laughter would fill the house and spill out into the street, where by now the young men of the village would have gathered. Bicycles would be shared, favourites got first choice sitting on the cross bar, and off they would go happy and carefree to enjoy whatever the night had to offer.

CHAPTER 6

THE MISSION

FOR WEEKS PRIOR to the appearance of the missionaries our parish priest would remind us every Sunday of our duty to attend the mission. The children of the area looked forward to it for it was the greatest event in our young lives. The spiritual side we did not understand too much. The attraction was the stalls.

The stall-holders came days before to be ready for the great event, when every household added another pious object to its already varied collection. Daily mass was a must for that fortnight and we children, who had to be practically dragged from our slumbers for school, were at the mission well in advance of our parents. Much to the annoyance of our teachers we had eyes only for the stalls. They were like an Aladdin's cave: beautiful statues of all the saints, Sacred Heart pictures, medals, scapulars, prayer books, little prayer cards. And the rosaries; now these were every child's delight. Such beautiful colours, they hung from hooks from the top of every stall, swinging in the breeze. We children would lovingly touch and secretly covet these lovely objects, extolling their praises to the stall-holder, who must have had the patience of Job, as we did not have any money.

This event happened every five years and as I grew into adulthood, the mission took on a different aspect. The priests came to help save our souls from damnation and they preached fire and brimstone. All the youngsters would know in advance when the sermon on company-keeping was imminent. Company-keeping was a sin unless the couple intended to marry and many a fine romance ended prematurely with that night's preaching. Queues for the confessionals were only seen at mission times and you quaked with fear in anticipation of what was to befall you once that confessional box door closed behind you.

The sexes were segregated: there was 'men's week' and 'women's week'. We girls would ask our brothers what the missionaries preached to them, but they would say that they were bound not to divulge their secrets and that anyway it was men's affairs and not for women's ears. So we would keep our own secrets when our turn came.

I used to imagine that we were all destined for eternal damnation, as so many thoughts, words and deeds were sins. But in spite of this, the mission was a wonderful social occasion and the women all enjoyed the gossip that ensued once their spiritual obligations were fulfilled.

The longer you stayed in the confessional, the greater the sinner everyone knew you were. It would be the general topic of conversation for months afterwards as to what penance was given to such a one. Of course, people always exaggerated and our local wit had a field day spreading these fabrications.

The makers of our 'mountain dew' – *poteen* – were noted for their excellence, but as it was an illegal brew, as far as the missionaries were concerned, these breakers of the laws of God and man were already damned. The purveyors of evil had to answer to God for the ruin of souls through drink and the missionaries would demand that their accursed stills should be brought into the church to be confiscated.

The owners of the tools of Satan would come like thieves in the darkness of night and drop the pieces of twisted metal over the church wall to be collected and displayed at the back of the church for all eyes to witness and condemn. Eventually the stills would be rendered unusable. There would be no more night fires in the bowels of the mountain until life reverted to its old form – generally a few months after the departure of the missionaries. Then you would see those same distillers at dusk, setting off for their old haunts like prospectors, with the tools of their trade on their backs, to be lost in the mists of the mountains.

The greatest sin of all was missing mass, which very few

people dared to do as they would be the talk of the parish. But there is always one who will go his own way regardless of neighbours, and he happened to live across the field from us. One of the missionaries regarded it as his duty to save Pakey's soul and tried to visit him several times – which was a rare event in our locality as our humble abodes were not deemed worthy of a visit from a priest, except in dire circumstances, such as a death.

Our house was the first dwelling the eye beheld on entering the village, but our dog, Prince, was aware of any stranger's presence well before he came into view. He sat on the highest vantage point outside our house and saw everything that went on for miles around. The priest was met and escorted with the frantic barking and growling by Prince, who was fiercely defensive of his castle. Cuchulain could not have done better. In the meantime, Pakey would hear the commotion, which was his cue to run for cover. One of us children would be delegated to help the priest find his quarry, but our lips were sealed as we had heard the stories of past informers in our unfortunate country and the punishment eventually meted out to them and their descendants.

Eventually the missionaries departed for fresh pastures. Looking back, they did help sustain the seeds sown in the soil of our souls of a faith to be ever grateful for. People benefitted morally and spiritually and it was also a break from the general routine of the endless work on the small hill-farms and a great get-together for all.

CHAPTER 7

PAT AND MARY

P AT AND MARY, a brother and sister, were our immediate neighbours. Although in my young days I never thought of them as such, they were like an extension of our family. Their house was a refuge when we incurred the wrath of our parents or older members of our family. We would go to them to tell our tale of woe and stay until we thought tempers had cooled. Their thatched house was set back off the road, about five minutes' walk from us up the boreen (lane).

We had no spring-well on our land but we were always welcome to use Mary and Pat's well. As we needed plenty of spring water, our trips past their house were many. We would enquire if they wanted anything from the shop and bring them the newspapers as they very rarely went to town.

Mary never married. She would laughingly say, 'Nobody ever asked me,' and Pat dared not bring another woman in as

Mary was a very strong character and, as he often said, there would be ructions in the house with two women. Nevertheless, I never heard a wrong word between them.

They were the possessors of one goose, and one or another member of our family would be promised the first egg, depending on the help we had given in their fields. We had an idea when that lovely white goose was about to deliver and this would be, as Pat had said, 'When her belly touches the ground and you see her wandering around like a lost soul. That's when she's looking for a nesting site.'

Several of us children accompanied her on her excursions and eventually she deposited her big, pure-white egg on top of the manure pit. She made the weirdest noises when trying to lay but we never gave her the chance to admire the fruits of her labour. The egg-saucepan was ready on the hot coals to receive the long-awaited prize, and several pairs of eyes watched as the water bubbled and danced in merriment as if aware of its part in this great ceremony. Pat would time it on his fob watch and it was the longest twelve minutes of that day.

The big egg-cup would be ceremoniously brought from the high shelf of the dresser, and the topping of the egg would begin. This was Mary's job. The egg would be tapped all around and then a clean cut made with a knife. The top was awarded to the youngest member of our family, and then we would eagerly watch the recipient dip into the golden well and we would plead for a spoonful of the mouthwatering meal. Pat would say that one goose egg was equal to a half-pound steak and we believed him. He also said that it took a strong stomach to eat one and if we suffered from tummy-ache, it was no use our mother coming complaining. If we had the ache afterwards, we always suffered in silence.

Pat and Mary also had a goat, Jenny, which they kept tethered, and it was my brother's job to change her and her tethering post to a new location when she had eaten everything within range. He was promised a kid if she ever had twins, which she eventually did. Then much to my mother's horror, he became the proud possessor of Janey.

Janey had to be bottle fed and was kept in a box beside the fire. She kept the whole house awake for weeks with her continuous bleating, but undaunted, my brother slept on a makeshift bed beside her until she settled. As she grew older she wandered in and out of the house. She thought she was human. She would take tit-bits from our hands at meal times and was greatly loved by everyone – until she did the unforgivable.

We had recently acquired a modern piece of furniture, a wardrobe with a full-length mirror on the outside. This was purchased for the benefit of a visitor from the USA. Janey was by now fully grown and sporting a strong pair of horns. She used to wander about our house, as was her right, or so she thought. She spotted her reflection in the new contraption and without

PAT AND MARY

more ado charged this impudent intruder into her precious domain.

Janey was banished as far away from the house as possible, leaving the cracked mirror behind. My mother said it was a bad omen and cried for her much-admired possession. My brother cried for his Janey. Eventually she sealed her own fate: she broke free from her tethered prison and bounced across the fields and garden, eating the bark off our young trees that were just beginning to mature. When the buyer came from the town to take Janey away, it was like a funeral. We could be heard throughout the village crying. We never owned a goat again.

Pat always wore wellingtons. I think they were a perk that went with his part-time job as a ganger-man for the county council. He was also issued with a three-quarter-length black coat and a waterproof cape. The wellies he wore all year round, which saved him quite a bit in shoe leather. He would go off for some months every year to supervise the building of roads. He travelled the three counties in his time, or so he said: Mayo, Galway, and Roscommon. When he came home for the winter he would be filled to the brim with all kinds of stories, especially ghost stories, and we would eagerly await his return. At dusk every evening he would be on our doorstep regardless of what household duties went on around him. He would sit on the furm (a long, narrow bench) beside the settle-bed and regale us with stories from his wanderings. We all used to be terrified as his ghost stories were hair-raising. He was always chewing tobacco and spitting his chew at anything in sight. My mother had to cover everything, especially anything cooking by the fire, as Pat was not too particular where he aimed.

By this time we had acquired two dogs, Monty and Goering. Goering was a bit weighty and Pat would abuse this poor animal, telling him that he was a good for nothing, fat, greedy so-and-so, and he would eventually get his come-uppance, like his namesake, the German. Goering would lie with his head on his paws, his sorrowful eyes directed at his aggressor. Pat would then aim his chewed tobacco spittle at the dog's eye and it would invariably hit its target, stinging and burning. The dog would run yelping from the house and lie by the hay-rick until the pain eased. Eventually when Goering heard Pat's footstep he would slink from beside the fire with his tail between his legs and make for the garden.

Pat had some peculiar ideas. He did not own a clock; only a fob watch. This hung on the wall inside the settle-bed in the big kitchen. He would never change the time for spring or summer time because Pat reckoned that he was not going to confuse his watch, putting it back and forward. It had quite sufficient to do to tell the time. He also re-christened everyone in the area and would tell us to say hello to people as they were passing. Of course, we did as we were told and did not realize, until we got a cuff on the ear, that we had called them by their nickname.

The names were not always complimentary – many were taken from prominent figures in the Boer War such as Kruger, Jobert and Cronje – but Pat would keep on smiling and chewing while we got into trouble.

On Christmas night we would hang up our stockings by their chimney and Santa always obliged. We would get some raisins, maybe an orange and always a new penny. I don't know how they managed to find a bright, shining penny. Mary's explanation was that Father Christmas was warned well in advance and that he had these coins specially minted. Oh, what lovely white lies; and we believed every word.

There was an odd job man in our area named Henry. He was homeless and harmless, but a good worker and always managed to get temporary work. He was also supplied with meals. If he was in our immediate locality he would take temporary accommodation at Pat and Mary's. They never turned him away. He would lie full-stretch on the furm and come bed-time he would remain there, and they would put the lamp out and go to bed. To make matters worse, Henry had a war wound that never healed. People used to say it was a legacy from a skirmish with the Black-and-Tans. At times the leg smelled terrible but Pat and Mary didn't seem to mind, although Pat called him a stinker behind his back.

Our visits were less frequent when Henry was in residence. We wondered if Henry ever heard the ghost that haunted one of the rooms in Pat and Mary's house. It was never spoken of, but the room was never used. We had daringly looked through the keyhole expecting, I suppose, to see something but there were just cobwebs everywhere and part of the ceiling had fallen in. The room was always locked. This was accepted by us and the neighbours as many houses were part-occupied by unearthly spirits.

When we asked the reason for these hauntings we were told that some people met untimely deaths, or that they had to come back to do restitution for some misdeed, or they died with sins on their souls and it should be a lesson to us to always follow God's laws. After mass on Sundays, three Hail Marys were always offered by priest and congregation for the benefit of these wandering souls.

CHAPTER 8

THE SISTERS

I N OUR VILLAGE of Treanoughter there were nine houses. We were the first house as you entered by road. If you happened to come across the hills then the first abode that greeted the eye was Durkin's. Three sisters lived here with their brother. They were all unmarried and they all looked the same age – ancient.

The sisters' mode of dress had not changed since the beginning of the century; long, calico-like skirts, usually black with dark, long-sleeved blouses, hand-made of course. Around the house they wore knitted shawls, but for outdoor wear it was a heavy, tasselled shawl that was worn over the head and wrapped around the upper part of the body. Their footwear was also from the past; high, brogue-type boots laced around little buttons, eyelets they called them, that reached midway up the calf of the leg and were hand-made by their brother John. Winnie, Mary and Murriah were their names and Winnie used to wear pieces of heather through her earlobes as earrings. I once asked her why she wore heather and she said that it was supposed to improve the eyesight.

Mass was their only outing apart from helping generally around their hill farm, but they lived comfortably and were self-sufficient. John went to town now and again to fairs or with produce. He would pass by our house with his ass and cart. He never made idle conversation. Just bade you the time of day, which usually was, 'Good-day to ye', and went about his business. He never owned or used a bicycle. He said he was not interested in these newfangled contraptions, but people knew the sisters ruled the roost and in their estimation anything new was thought up by the devil to lead people astray. Nevertheless their little home with its thatched roof was like a paradise, sitting high up in the hills with a panoramic view of the countryside.

Visitors were not encouraged, especially children. We generally got as far as the half-door and they talked out to us as they busied themselves, polishing and cleaning and cooking. They were like ants, forever going hither and thither, needing approval from each other for everything they did. They would tolerate your questions for so long and then tell you to be going home to your mother. They lived in peaceful isolation, untouched by the stresses of the outside world. The only house they visited was their married sister's, halfway down the village.

THE SISTERS

Kate had married Ned MacHugh late in life, much to her family's bewilderment, and was as industrious as her maiden sisters. Her husband, Ned, was a quiet man with odd ways. He used to talk loudly to himself and we would invite ourselves into his house just to watch his antics.

A boiled egg was a luxury in most houses in those days, as eggs were used as barter for household goods bought from the travelling shop, which was a horse-drawn, caravan-type vehicle that toured the villages on a certain day of the week. It was a Godsend for the people, especially the housebound, as they would otherwise have been unable to buy the necessities without having to haul their eggs to the shop, which was some distance away.

Ned liked a boiled egg every day. This could be eaten at any time: maybe for his dinner, as they ate simply. He had the peculiar habit of walking around his kitchen while he ate the egg, his hob-nailed boots beating like clap-hammers on the flagstoned floor. If the weather was inclement Ned would be wearing his cloak. It was the original *breide* or frieze coat worn by all men in time past around the countryside. It was bestowed on a man when he was full-grown and lasted all his life. Ned was still the proud possessor of this garment, the only one in the locality. It reached to the ankles and was sleeveless, with a clasp at the neck and waist which could be fastened.

Kate had knitted a type of pixie hat to protect his head and ears from the blistering winds that blew down from the mountains and hills. Ned looked like a cross between a mad monk and a hangman as he trampled around the house, proclaiming to us the importance of eating an egg in this manner, waving his knife in the air between mouthfuls of this delicacy. He reckoned that spoons were for children. He would then fill his enamel mug with spring water and drink his fill, which he maintained was food for the gods. He would instill in us the need to drink plenty of milk as we were growing.

His wife would take no notice of this activity, but would carry on with her household duties. She had probably become accustomed to his unusual behaviour. We would go home and relate everything we had seen, but my mother would say that God put all sorts on the earth and so long as they harmed no-one then they were entitled to their odd ways.

The sisters always collected their dear Katie for last mass on Sunday when all the chores were finished. The four would then wind their way slowly down the back bog road to the church, like old ladies that had stepped out of a picture-book.

Katie had a profound limp from an accident when she was a child. She had fallen awkwardly from a hay cart and dislocated her hip. It went unnoticed until it was too late. When medical help was sought in our villages, this would usually be the bone-setter quack, as he was called, who did his best, but often did more harm than good. People placed a lot of trust in those people, however, and someone usually had a cure for most ailments. Their help was always free as money was scarce and doctors cost money.

Eventually the journey to the church became too strenuous for the two older sisters, and that was the last contact with the outside world severed. Then came a visit from distant relatives from Yorkshire, England. These long-lost cousins were a nine-day wonder and we used to follow them far up the boreen, intrigued with their foreign lingo. We could not understand one word they said. The sisters themselves were impressed with their relations and seemed to enjoy the excitement they caused in our ordinary everyday village life. In fact things were never the same again in that little house on the hillside.

It was clear that the visitors had broken the barrier between centuries when Winnie arrived at mass with stud earrings instead of heather, and a coat and hat instead of a shawl, although she still wore the same long skirt and high boots. The mists of time had lifted and the twentieth century had come to take the sisters where they had previously been frightened to venture. Even bicycles were acquired with money from the relatives. John never learned to ride his two-wheeled monster, but they were very handy for the visitors when they came every year to enjoy a peaceful interlude in this little haven on the hill in Treanoughter, with its thatched roof and whitewashed walls, with pots of geraniums adorning the outside sills of every window.

CHAPTER 9

DENNIS AND HIS MOUNTAIN DEW

H IGH IN THE hills at the end of our village lived four families. The road leading to their homes was so steep that no donkey was expected to pull a loaded cart to the top. Turf had to be stacked at the butt of the hill, and each family carried their precious fuel in sacks on their backs to their hilltop homes.

Unlike the rest of the village, where the whitewashed thatched cottages were scattered about, the four houses on this little plateau were in close proximity to each other.

In a slated house sharing a spectacular view with their three neighbours lived the Malone family: Dennis, his two brothers, sister and elderly mother. Their modern residence was acquired through the generosity of a relative in America who had, so the story goes, made his money bootlegging. The distilling of illegal brews was practised both sides of the Atlantic. Dennis was renowned for his *poteen*.

In times past the family used to brew away in the hills well off the beaten track. But Dennis was so bold as to defy both neighbours and the law by using an outhouse for this purpose. Living in the crow's-nest, as he called his part of the village, he could spot strangers miles away, and lookouts would be posted in advantageous positions when the brewing was in session. His dog, Spot, would be tied on top of the hill with a clear view of anyone using the old paths. He was trained to give timely warning. The *Gardai* (police) sometimes used the same old paths on raids, and this canine sleuth had an aversion towards anyone in uniform. When he saw them, he would set up a wail that would awaken the dead. All work in the village would cease and the speculations were immense as the *Gardai* searched high and low for Dennis's home-made whiskey. The whiff of the brew assailed the *Gardai*'s nostrils as they crossed the hills, but finding it was another problem.

I remember one harvest-time when everyone was working all the daylight hours to get the corn in from the fields. We saw great activity on the hill and realised that a raid was imminent. We were also aware from the smell which had lingered in the air for days that the newly distilled harvest-brew was ready. However, Spot the dog, tied in his usual place on the hill, had eaten through his rope as the scent of romance came to him on the wind. He forgot he was on sentry-duty and off he went.

On this occasion the law had come in civvies so as not to

alert the lookouts. They were relieved to find the watch-dog, who had betrayed their presence previously, missing. They felt sure that this time they would nab the culprit, Dennis, and tip his brew into one of the many mountains streams that flowed past the houses down into the valley below. They converged on this seemingly peaceful part of our village, surrounding all the houses in case they were in neighbourly collusion.

The intruders were spotted in the nick of time. Dennis and his brothers, who had been bringing in corn to be stacked, placed the illicit brew and still in the middle of a stack and started building around the booty.

There were the *Gardai* frantically searching, aware that they would be the laughing-stock of the villagers if they were not successful. They climbed into lofts and looked under beds, searched every out-house and even looked in the milk-churns, while the householders looked on in amusement and shouted developments to the Malone family, busy at work in their haggard (stack-yard).

When the police finally went to search the haggard, there was Dennis diligently at work making a stack while his brother, Joe, casually forked the sheaves up to him, all the while chiding these dispensers of the law on the futility of their search and the waste of good government money, telling them they would be better occupied doing a hard day's work than harassing a hard-working family like themselves. Dennis could not resist telling them that as soon as they were out of sight he would change the buttermilk in the churns back into poteen. The *Gardai* went away dejected, with jeers ringing in their ears, knowing that once more Dennis had outwitted them.

The story of Dennis and the *Gardai* would be told and retold for months afterwards. But there were many women in the surrounding villages who would have been delighted if Dennis's activities were curtailed. Husbands and sons went under cover of darkness for the *poteen* and spent hard-earned money to the neglect of their families. The brew was so potent that a person became inebriated without realizing.

Dennis had no qualms as to who consumed the liquor. He was in this business for gain. He did not care when people said that the devil's child had the devil's luck, and that he would come to a bad end for tempting so many youths into drunken ways and fighting and carousing because the brew was so available.

Ned, one of Dennis's brothers, was disabled due to contracting polio as a child. He took an active part in delivering his brother's booty to the nearest town, where he had regular customers. Ned depended entirely on his ass and cart for transport, and when the day came that rubber wheels were available for carts he was the first to avail himself of those mod-cons. He would remove the front part of the box of his cart and sit with his lifeless leg dangling over the side and his crutches beside him.

The *Gardai* in that town never suspected this happy-go-lucky, cheerful young man, with a friendly word for everyone, to be trafficking in moonshine. He shared in the proceeds as he was a bit of a gambler and needed the money for his card-playing sessions.

Country people were keen card-players and they would travel miles, especially at Christmas, for a game of twenty-five. Ned seldom missed a game and he was never short of passengers in his ass-cart. The journey to and from these card games was enjoyed by all, and oft-times it would be the early hours of the morn before they got home. But they could sleep late once the harvest was safely in the haggard and potatoes and vegetables stored near the house. It was a time to relax and enjoy the fruits of the year's hard work.

Dennis was more interested in the ladies and would come through the village like a breeze of wind on his racing bicycle with hair sleeked back with brilliantine. He was a bit of a dandy and fancied himself as a lady-killer.

As he sped through the villages, he deprived many a household of a good laying hen and he would ride on with a curse ringing in his ears, usually 'Mallacht Cromwell ort' – 'the curse of Cromwell on you'. This meant that they hoped he would be made homeless. In fact, the reverse happened. He inherited a farm and dwelling-house from a bachelor uncle, married and settled down. Not having the protection of the hills any more and living with new neighbours, he hid the still away, to gather rust in the rafters of some outhouse. Never again did the breeze bring the smell of that rare old perfume from the hilltop to the people in the valley below.

CHAPTER 10

THE CAPTAIN

T HE EMPTY HOUSE stood in the middle of the wind-
swept landscape. It reminded me of a lonesome
orphan child waiting for someone to claim it. I used
to sit on the fence at the end of our garden opposite the
deserted dwelling, and wonder why someone could abandon
their home and disappear without tale or tidings for years. The
grown-ups refused any information about the owner when we
asked, always reprimanding us for being curious and telling us
we were too young to understand.

Then one day it was noticed that there was smoke coming
from the distant chimney, and all eyes in the village were
focused on that blue-green peat smoke rising to the heavens,
proclaiming to everyone that the owner was again in residence,
and the house alive once more.

Curiosity sent every villager within the next few days and

THE CAPTAIN

nights to the door of the returned exile, all bearing some edible offering, and the old familiar paths leading in different directions through the bogs again came alive to the tread of human feet.

Eventually I met the Captain, as he was now known, and heard the story of his years in exile. His land had been repossessed for a debt left unpaid by his aged parents, and as there was no work locally or elsewhere, he had to join the British Army. He served in India, and eventually rose to the rank of Captain. He came back and redeemed his precious piece of land, and many a happy hour my brother and I spent with him, listening to the tales of far-off places.

He never hankered after material things. The old dresser belonging to his parents still stood with just the bare essentials: one tin mug and plate and a clock, a settle-bed in the corner, a long, wooden furm alongside the bed and a few chairs.

At the end of the flagstoned kitchen was a cow-byre with channel and wooden manger, a relic of bygone times when man and beast shared the same dwelling.

The ticking of the clock in this emptiness could be heard before you entered the house, and the echo of the Captain's footsteps as he swept the imaginary dust off his shining flagstones. He used to say that during his exile he used to visualise opening his own door and walking the flagstones to his own hearth. He used to long for the smell of the peat smoke and

6 9

missed all the lovely things he took for granted growing up, like the sound of the river that flowed close by, rushing on its way into the lake.

The Captain was a tall man, well over six feet, clean-shaven and straight as a ramrod. In summer he would shave outside his house, a mirror hanging from a tree. We used to watch, fascinated, as he sharpened his cut-throat razor on the leather strap that hung on the side of the dresser. He would lather his face from a stick of soap which he kept in a silver-like box, with a separate box for his lathering brush, a legacy from his army days, I suppose.

When we killed a goose we would bring him a jar of goose-fat for his boots to make them water-proof and keep the leather supple. When my mother went to town shopping, she would buy him some delicacy, usually *barm-brac* (fruit loaf). He also loved herrings so he got a share of ours. We never went to his house empty-handed. We would bring him a bottle of milk, and sometimes he would give me a penny. He had a peculiar habit of wrapping it in strips of paper which he wound around and around the penny until it looked ten times its original size. He always did this in the parlour, which was bare except for a table. He would shut the door, and the noise from the tearing of the paper sounded from the empty room as if he were tearing calico.

His land and surroundings were a natural habitat for all

wild creatures, and he jealously guarded this sanctuary. He never encumbered himself with any domestic animals or availed himself of any of the many pets, cats and dogs, that kindly neighbours encouraged him to keep. He never tilled his soil again, but leased it and was glad of the company of the people who worked on it

He used to bring us to see the ruins of a church that stood near the lake shore and told us it was a holy place. We would sit in the ruins and listen enthralled to the story of the plunder of that same little stone church. How the British soldiers in the penal days hid in the woods nearby and watched the villagers wind their various ways to mass through the bogs and across the fields, following the old paths, some to cross the river by the well-known stepping-stones. Mass was forbidden but people still hid their priest, who had to be educated in Europe and would return to travel the country in disguise, saying mass wherever possible.

While mass was in progress the soldiers burst in and massacred the people, who had formed a barrier to protect the priest. He got away through a trap door at the back of an altar, which had a tunnel to near the lake, where a boat was harboured ready for a quick getaway. But the boat was also under surveillance by the enemy, so the priest, with the chalice and consecrated hosts, rushed in desperation towards the lake itself, with the soldiers in hot pursuit. Miraculously, steps appeared out of the lake before him, then disappeared as he sped onwards across them. Eventually he stood, apparently on the water, safe in the middle of the lake and the soldiers were dumbfounded. They abandoned their quarry, knowing that a miracle had happened in front of their eyes. The priest was later rescued by boat and taken to a safe place. This story was well-known around our locality, and we would reverently look out over the peaceful waters of the lake and wonder at the glorious part it had played in our darkest days.

We were allowed into the Captain's woods once a year to pick nuts, but we were forever watchful in case the spirits of the soldiers still lurked in this lonely area, where only the birds and animals now reigned supreme. We were the only family of children allowed in this dark, forbidding place. He would say we had to be quiet so as not to frighten the wildlife. The lonesome cooing of the doves could be heard deep in the woods, and as we picked the nuts they would scare us by their flutterings through the trees, protesting at being disturbed. Human beings rarely visited their dwelling place.

The Captain would also tell us tales of bygone days and forbade us to go near a certain field of his where the fairies held court at night in their fort. This 'fort' was a circular earthwork mound with a large flat stone covering an opening in its floor. Little did he know we were scared even to look in its direction, as we were warned from infancy what would befall us if we dared set foot in that forbidden ground. The whirlwind that was familiar in our part of the country was supposed to be fairy magic that swept you to their palace, for they were always looking for mortals to help them reign in their kingdom. If you did not spit three times into the fairy wind, you would disappear forever into the enchanted land of the little people.

CHAPTER 11

THE
BOGEY MAN

I HAD WANDERED AWAY from home. I must have been getting venturesome as I had climbed a gate and gone into a field that was forbidden to us children. It had been reclaimed from the wild surroundings and, where the gorse and bushes once reigned supreme, now bloomed in all their glory the lovely white and yellow flowers of masses of Kerrs Pink potatoes. Then I heard the frightened call of my mother, screeching like a mother-hen calling her brood together when danger was near, 'The bogey man; the bogey man. Come in and close the door, quick.' In all the excitement I was not missed, but I could see, and indeed knew instinctively, that the bogey man was on his way.

I did not know then if he was man or phantom. I imagined that he materialized from the bend in the road where one caught the first glimpse of man or beast coming into our village.

Panic set in. I was in his direct path, as before the road was made this was the highway used by all and sundry. I heard our gate creak. He was taking the short cut. I was doomed: would I die straight away, or would I have to wander forever with the bogey man through the hills and dales of Ireland, through a faceless land where every household shut its door as he passed, as if he would taint them with some terrible plague?

I tried to climb the high, sod ditch that was once the dividing-line between bog and garden before the Land Commission gave grants for the reclamation of *shroid*, or rough land. It was like trying to conquer Everest. The more I tried to climb, the more panic stricken I became. I slid down with my fingers full of earth, my eyes blinding with tears of despair, my clothes soiled with the contact of body and earth, the earth I would gladly have melted into if possible. Eventually I could try no more; my child's strength was spent and I was ready to meet my fate. I felt I was paralysed and then I saw this apparition standing over me. It must be the bogey man.

I could see a bearded face, dishevelled hair, clothes stained with grass and soil and sand. The thing had a human voice and spoke in soft tones to me. Was I dreaming? But no! This dreaded bogey man was picking me up and hoisting me on to the top of the fence into my garden, all the time scolding the silly mother who had allowed a little girl to wander into a place where there was so much deep water. The archives of my mind refuse to release the happenings of the remainder of that day, but years afterwards I heard the sad story of the bogey man, Jack Egan.

He was once a happy husband and father on a small farm in the next village to ours. In those days the men of the area were migratory workers – *spalpeens*, as they were known. They would go to certain farm areas of England, and in the towns the hirers would converge to choose their workers for the season. Prices would be settled and the *spalpeens* would accompany their new masters, some to work like slaves in the worst conditions possible, until their contract was complete.

It was on a Yorkshire farm that Jack got the news of his only child's death, as did many other fathers. The dreaded plague, diptheria, was raging through Ireland. It was like the massacre of the innocents. Most families suffered the loss of one or more children: my own three-year-old elder sister was one of them. The tragedy of losing his son unhinged this poor father, and he never accepted the fact that his little one would not be there when he eventually returned home.

The homecomings, which were always a joyous occasion, were dreaded that year, and Jack thought he would bury his troubles by drinking himself into a stupor for days on end. In his despair he blamed his wife for neglecting their child. He could not accept the terrible ill-fortune that life had dealt him and inevitably his marriage floundered. Came the time he did not stumble into view any more, and people probably did not mind too much as he reminded them of their own loss.

CHAPTER 12

THE HERMIT

W E HAD TO pass his house on our way to and from school. He was nameless. Everyone referred to him as the hermit. So far as we were concerned he was also faceless, as never a glimpse of him did we get. We were warned to give his place a wide berth, and anyone would think the devil was in hot pursuit as we raced past his boreen like the hammers of hell, always fearful of an unseen hand reaching out to drag us into this Godforsaken no-man's-land.

To us children a hermit could be anything, and our imagination ran riot as we listened to strange stories told around the fire on a winter's night. He was supposed to be in league with the 'Fella Below'. Satan was seldom mentioned by name in case you might incur his wrath. Others would claim that he had willingly handed over his residence to the fairies to come and go as they pleased, and they, in turn protected him and supplied him with the necessities of life; so woe betide any child daring to step beyond this boundary.

The storyteller would then relate unusual past happenings to his eager audience. How the Hermit had the power to charm the birds into his walled garden and that he could converse with them. That was one of the stories that fired my imagination, and as I got a little older I became more daring. I resolved to sneak a look into this forbidden territory. Memory evades me as to the events leading up to this eventful day in my life, although I can recall vividly certain scenes, as from a play. A child sitting on a high wall looking into an enchanted garden, feasting her eyes on the beautiful flowers that grew in profusion with gay abandon everywhere. Trees laden with fruit. Gooseberry bushes so heavy with offspring that they bowed to the ground as if curtseying to the flowers. It was no great wonder that the birds flocked to this beautiful paradise and nested there unmolested, their music echoing through the trees as each bird lent its note of gladness.

I was so overawed by this magical sight that I failed to see the Hermit until he was directly beneath where I was sitting. He looked like a man but he was so small. His features I could not determine as grey, matted hair sprouted from everywhere; even out of his ears. He walked with the aid of a walking stick, and suddenly it dawned on me who he was. This was 'Sean Matthais', Old Matthew, the old man from the Irish book I was reading at school. The description fitted him perfectly. He roared at me, demanding an explanation as to who I was and why I was trespassing on his property, frightening his little friends the *eanini*, the birds. He spoke in Irish. With every bellow he hit the wall with his stick. I tried to tell him my name, 'Maura Cait,' but the word failed to materialize. Sheer horror gripped me and rendered me dumb.

He shouted, 'Come down here.' How could I? My eyes magnified the distance between us. I sat there mesmerized like the little red hen in my first story book. Old Matthew was the fox, and I knew the inevitable would happen. I would fall off my perch like the little red hen, to be carried away by the wily fox.

True to the story book, it happened, and there I was in a heap at his feet. The power of speech had returned, probably with the shock of the fall. I was begging for mercy. 'Sean Matthais, I promise I will never frighten your friends again. Please let me go home.'

'Why are you calling me Sean Matthais? That's not my name.'

So I told him the story from my Irish book at school – *Isogan*, 'Jesus' – about the old man whom people said had sold his soul to the devil, just as the village storyteller had said of him. That children used to steal into his garden through a hole in the wall and play there with the birds and climb the trees without their parents knowing. Then one day the children came to where 'Old Matthais' was sitting under his favourite apple tree, asking for his help, as one of their number was stuck on a branch above where he was sitting. Old Matthais put up his arms to take the child and the enormous weight forced the old man to the ground. He was amazed, until the child said, 'You had the weight of the sins of the world in your arms.' It was Jesus playing in his garden.

The old man, Roger as he was really called, sat down and thanked me for the wonderful story with tears streaming down his face and weaving little rivulets through his beard. He had never learned to read as the hedgerow schoolmaster had to have some form of payment, and maybe his parents could not afford this, so he was denied the pleasure of becoming lost in another world between the covers of a book. He had always avoided children as he spoke only Irish and thought they would not be able to understand him. Once he realized that we could converse with him, he was delighted.

As the local children began to lose their fear of him we would be allowed to play in his garden, but we were never invited into his house. We would fill ourselves in due season with cherries, gooseberries and apples, while he listened, enthralled, to the simple, childish stories we read to him in Irish. He, in turn, would regale us with songs and stories of bygone days. He never did associate with grown-ups but became as one of us children, and I like to think that *Isogan* 'Jesus' really came to play in his garden.

THE HERMET

The boreen leading to Roger's house was a link with the past, as the flagstones that formed the path were laid by the first owners and now worn smooth by the constant comings and goings of a people long since dead. The briars grew and entwined themselves around the drystone walls that snaked their way on each side of the boreen up to the little thatched cottage. As we walked or ran on these flagstones, our steps were amplified, as if an underground chamber existed beneath. It was very eerie, but one of our favourite pastimes once we had made friends with Roger.

The cottage was hidden from view by the massive trees that stood sentinel over the old man's abode, as if protecting him from the outside world. Little wisps of smoke escaped from the chimney, trying to reach the sky, but were prevented by the trees that joined hands around the house as if playing ring-a-ring-a-roses. The blue, hazy smoke spread its mantle over the surroundings like a perpetual mist. It was an ideal setting for Sleeping Beauty; but only poor old Roger lived there, locked in time and memory of bygone days.

The first time I ventured into his house I heard the cows lowing continuously in the middle of the day, which was most unusual. I knocked on the door but there was no answer, so I lifted the old, rickety latch, and gently pushed it open. The stench from inside made me gasp and I fell into cow's dung that was heaped high. It was like taking a trip into another era as

Roger still had the cows in stalls at the end of his house. It was a legacy from the past when harsh laws prevented the keeping of more than one animal, and to add insult to injury, a barn, or outhouse was taxed, so the poor down-trodden peasant had to share his roof with animals: the fowls in a loft over the cow, which was a necessity for milk.

Roger was ill in his settle-bed close to his three cows. He asked if I would go to the spring-well as he had not had a drink for days. The cows also wanted water. I lit a fire and made some tea and Roger kept muttering in Irish, '*Ta-an tart mor-orm*,' – 'The big thirst is on me,' meaning death was beckoning. I went home to fetch my mother and brothers and in a few hours the cows were milked, the cow dung cleared to the manure heap and the house generally tidied up.

We got his permission to send for the doctor. There were no phones in those days, so it was a cycle ride of five miles to the nearest town for one of my brothers. The doctor arrived and as Roger had not any relatives to care for him, he was removed to hospital. The doctor did not have a great command of Irish, so I was translating. I had to inform Roger that a visit from the priest was necessary, or so the doctor said. Roger said, 'Tell that physician of the body that I can look after my own soul and anyway, the priest probably can't hear confessions in Irish so if I've got any sins to confess, that's between myself and the Man Above.'

So Roger went to hospital and after some time he improved

a little. A woman neighbour in our own village, who had visited him in hospital, took him to her home and cared for him until he died in the winter.

I never again laid eyes on my old friend 'Sean Matthais' – Old Matthew as I first believed him to be – but I remember hearing people talk about his death: that his body lay in an outhouse for three weeks owing to the bad weather. It was the year of the big snow and the roads were impassable. Our village was cut off from the outside world for weeks. I remember seeing his coffin pass by our house, the men of the village carrying it on their shoulders through the snow, men in front sounding out the surface of the road and men walking behind ready to take over as others got tired. We shook holy water on his little coffin and bade him goodbye in Irish and begged God's mercy on his soul.

When the snow had cleared, the priest and some neighbours went to the graveyard for the blessing of the grave, and his mortal remains were laid to rest properly. The good lady who had cared for him in his illness inherited his property and sold it eventually. Within twelve months a new house stood in one of his fields. The dry stone walls were razed to the ground and a brand new gravel road now covered the old flagstones. The trees that grew unhindered for centuries were mercilessly chopped down, and Roger's old homestead was now a bare piece of ground where hens scratched and pigs foraged. The children going to and from school had now got another interest: the two children who lived in this new house with their parents. We made friends with the family and we, in turn, used to tell them stories about Roger, our friend.

CHAPTER 13

TOM AND
SLIPPY

T HE HOUSE THAT Tom Lynch and Slippy, his father, occupied was known locally as the house at the butt of the hill. This was in the most beautiful setting, sheltered by *Mulloch Buide* (Yellow Hill, or summit) on one side, with trees all around it, and a stream nearby which connected the two lakes which were within two minutes walk of the house. This abode with its scenic surroundings could have been the dwelling-place of princes, but alas, these two inhabitants were more like paupers.

There was never much activity around this so-called farmhouse, as father and son slept while others toiled. The cows were left unmilked and lowing in their barns, the manure heaped practically up to the animals' tails. In passing we would lift the latch and tell Tom that the cows were losing their milk and he would say, 'Well then, that will save me having to milk them,' and he would slumber on.

In summer the air was perfumed by the fragrant smell of the yellow whins which grew in profusion on the hill overlooking the house. It was a glorious sight to behold this golden mass of blossom. Their exhilarating scent would invade the nostrils, and we would fill our lungs to bursting with the perfume which nature had provided. The whins were home and sustenance to myriads of winged creatures. We used to sit and watch and listen to the grasshoppers in their coats of green, clicking like mini threshing machines as they foraged among the whins. There were also birds galore.

This hill also had other inhabitants: badgers, foxes and rabbits, plus a demon of a mule named Browney. He belonged to Tom and was as lazy as his master. The mule spent most of his time devising means of scaring all the local children. As the main road passed immediately under the hill, he would lie in wait for us among the whins. We would try to sneak past, but this genderless son of Satan would dart from his hiding place and kick his back-legs in the air, making a soulless noise, a cross between a neigh and a bray. He would show us his discoloured teeth, which were like piano keys, and run along the path at the foot of the hill, threatening to come out and devour us.

I feel sure he had a vendetta against nature for having allowed him to be born with no certain species to be identified with, and unable ever to reproduce. His sole purpose in life was to deprive all mothers of their offspring. He was well fed as he

TOM AND SLIPPY

had practically all the fields to wander through at will. The cows were never allowed to graze at the same time in the same pasture as this cantankerous animal. The only time he was imposed on was for a foray into the bogs with his master, usually at night, to relieve some unsuspecting owner of a good cartload of turf, which was usually stacked by the side of the road for winter to sell in the town. It was a great source of income for some families, but Tom and his mule delighted in their nightly excursions and were quite particular as to the quality of their ill-gotten goods. Then their fire would burn brightly and when people went to visit, they would recognize the fruits of their hard labour giving warmth and pleasure to those two who slept the best part of their lives away.

The people in our locality were of a gentle nature so they tolerated these two misfits. Their house needed thatching but they did not bother. The walls were discoloured from rain. My brother and I would go in, especially when it was raining, and we would watch, fascinated, as the raindrops played little tunes as they tinkled into every known receptacle. These were dotted around the floor to receive their watery guests, who came in uninvited through the roof and eventually overflowed and left through the door.

Every summer we would ask Slippy for his permission to cut loads of whins and draw them by the cartload to our farm-house to act as barriers between fields and hens. These free-range scratters would ruin the growing grain if some obstacle was not put in their way, and the thorny whins were the best deterrent. The fences around our house and fields were bedecked with these golden garlands, the aroma permeating both house and barns. Some of our wily hens would take flight and get to the forbidden grain, then they would have their wings clipped. Eventually the whins would wither and dry like tinderwood and they would then be taken to a safe place and burned. By this time the crops would be harvested and the hens allowed into the fields to gorge themselves on the left-overs.

Slippy, known as Slippycoat, was the oldest man in our parish at that time and a great historian and story-teller. He got his nickname from a coat he used to wear. People referred to it as a claw-hammered coat. It was made of a shiny material, probably silk, and he also wore a top hat. It looked so out of place in a farming community, where people wore corduroy breaches and home-spun jerseys, and caused a lot of mirth amongst the villagers, but Slippy did not care.

In his younger days he spent some years away from home and he travelled widely, or so he said. Rumour had it that he was batman to an officer in the British army and he used to tell us about the places he had visited. Others said he was just a butler in a gentleman's house and that he had never left Ireland. We did not mind as he used to tell us such wonderful stories, and when he came to cut wild grass and rushes that grew along the river near our home, we were there eager to help. We would make *sugans* (straw ropes) from our own stacks of straw to tie up his bundles, and when he had finished he would sit on the flag-stones that formed the end part of the bridge which scaled the river and take his shoes off, and we would all sit with our feet dangling in the water listening to his wonderful songs and stories.

As it got dark we would be called for bed, and we would hoist the bundles on Slippy's back and watch him disappear around the rock to be lost in the shadows, leaving us dreaming of far-off places and wondering if, indeed, the world was as big and exciting as he said.

Once, we were asked at school to gather some folklore from our part of the country. This was requested from Dublin. It was a country-wide project and there was a prize for the best stories gathered from each school. Needless to say, Slippy was my informant and I got the prize. This amassing of local history had to be censored by my elder brother, Michael, as Slippy was not too particular about his grammar.

One of the stories was about three tall stones which stood side-by-side on a sea shore somewhere in West Mayo. They were supposed to have once been the three sons of a mermaid. A fisherman used to watch the mermaid come in on the beach to comb her hair and fell in love with her. He decided to catch her. She could not go back to the sea without her net, which she always kept close beside her, so the fisherman captured the net and took the mermaid home to be his wife. He buckled her (had his way with her), and had three sons. (This is how Slippy told the story.) She was always homesick for the sea and one day, when the boys had grown up, she asked them to get the net from their father. Once she had the net in her possession again, she took the boys to the beach and turned them into stones as a punishment against their father for stealing her away from her home. Then the mother swam back to her own kind beneath the waves, leaving a stark reminder to others not to tangle with those people who prefer water to land.

I wondered why my brother crossed out 'buckled' and put 'fathered three sons'. As the teacher impressed upon us the need for clear and well-written work and examined the work as it came in, I explained that it was my brother who had crossed out the word and what it originally was. I got a whacking when I got home for mentioning such a word to the teacher, but of course I had had no idea of its indelicate meaning.

CHAPTER 14

KITTY
AND LARRY

T HE PLACE THAT Kitty and Larry D'Arcy called home was situated on the flat, high plateau above Slippy's hill. It commanded a view unparalleled for its beauty anywhere. Standing at their front door, the eyes of the beholders were dazzled with the scenery set out as if by an artist's hand. Nature had indeed endowed this part the countryside with a generous share of its bounty: lakes to the right and left, rivers and hills and mountains and dells, interspersed with sprinklings of whitewashed, thatched cottages. Only the turf smoke gently issuing from the chimneys, reminded the onlooker that this was not the enchanted land he or she might be imagining.

Time stood still in this once-happy home, especially for Kitty, as she had the unfortunate experience of being left at the altar by her husband-to-be. The man in question had disappeared the night before the wedding and emigrated to

England. He was never seen again. This sad episode left Kitty with her mind gone astray. She was so traumatized by the event that she refused to leave her home and was almost completely house-bound.

Local people said that she was once the prettiest girl in the neighbourhood, and indeed her now-faded looks were a testimony to that fact. Every now and then she would dress up in her pretty, but old, bonnet, with faded roses around the brim, put on the long, fitted coat, and gather her beaded string bag and gloves and start out for the church to get married, as she thought. Half way there, some long-distant memory of the betrayal would jolt her confused brain and send her back home weeping uncontrollably. She never passed through the door of that church again as she was incapable of sitting still for any length of time, and would not understand what was going on anyway. Time had no meaning for her. She rarely left her own hearth and never encouraged anyone to visit.

My brother and I wandered everywhere among the neighbours' houses, unmolested, and we would visit Kitty just to watch her bizarre rituals as she went about her daily chores. She would wash her hands incessantly, especially when baking bread. Instead of gathering the ingredients all together, she would collect the flour from its dry place beside the fire, wash her hands, go to the dresser for the baking soda, forget what she wanted and again wash her hands, shake her head from side to side and mutter something. This went on endlessly until some semblance of soda-bread went in the oven.

By this time we were mesmerized and so was Kitty, but we would still stay around to see the results of the baking. Usually a flat, hard piece of so-called bread was presented to us, while she would stand and watch and make us eat it. We were too frightened to do otherwise.

Another time we would go and visit and tell her it was Sunday when it was a weekday, and she would then get ready for mass and, escorted by three or four of us, would set off for the river. She never crossed the stepping-stones but knelt at the water's edge and made us do the same. She went through all the motions of hearing mass. Afterwards she nodded and conversed with invisible people. She would put her hand on our shoulders and introduce us, telling them we were her friends. We had to pretend they were really there. She would bid them all good-day and return home.

Our parents were not aware of what we were doing, but we never intended to cause Kitty any distress. It was as if we did not believe the grown-up stories about her, so we had to find out for ourselves.

Larry went about his work seemingly never noticing any oddity about his sister. He was now getting on in years so was not capable of doing hard farm work. He let his land in con-acre (an eleven-month lease), and our family usually renewed the lease year after year. The D'Arcys depended on this income, and we supplied them with some produce from their land. Larry also sold eating apples from his well-stocked orchard, and woe betide anyone caught stealing his precious fruit.

The cow's barn backed on to the orchard, and Larry would throw the cow manure through the opening in the wall. Because he was not tilling his land the manure was not used as fertilizer, so accumulated until the apple trees were hardly visible amid the dung-heaps. So the orchard benefited from an abundance of nutrients. Come autumn, the mouthwatering rosy apples would hang invitingly, just waiting to be plucked.

Temptation would overcome fear and each year we would make several attempts to deprive Larry of some of his luscious fruit. Sometimes we were successful and would hide our cache as far away from our home as possible, as we would be punished for stealing. We would tie a belt around our jumpers and pack the apples inside. But we became too daring, and one day my brother Tony and I were up in the branches of a tree, picking to our hearts' content as Kitty had told us that Larry had taken to his bed. We imagined him being ill but he was only having a nap. He appeared in the orchard with the pitchfork vowing vengeance on the thieves. He spotted my brother perched high in the branches, his jumper bulging with loot. He stood underneath and informed Tony in no uncertain terms what he would do when he got him on the ground: how he would use his cut-throat razor to relieve him of his vital organs. As for me, I was quaking with fear. He was telling me how I would be speared on top of his pitchfork. Larry was mumbling and dancing around like someone who had lost his wits.

Eventually we had to come down and meet our fate. I got stuck in the manure-heap under the tree as I was weighed down with apples and guilt. I lost my sandals and nearly lost my life as I was swallowed in this heaving mass of cow-dung.

We were relieved to have escaped his clutches but we had a far worse fate awaiting us when we got home. The loss of sandals and the ruining of clothes was a further drain on our household expenses and money was already scarce. My mother walloped us and had to wash me in the river from head to toe. I was threatened that I would have to go to school bare footed, and that was the greatest humiliation of all. The smell of cow dung clung to me for days and my brother and sisters seized on this as a time for some fun at my expense, urging my mother to banish me to the barn where I belonged. Never again did we dare steal Larry's apples. We had learned our lesson.

D'Arcy's house was once the most commodious thatched dwelling in the locality. In my mother's younger days, she and others from our village would be invited to the thriving and comfortable home with its flower garden and orchard and roses trailing around the doors and windows. The teachers from the local school used to lodge there and would join in the evening's entertainment. The family were blessed with the gift of music and played several instruments between them.

Local folklore told of an ancestor of the D'Arcy family who had helped a stranger who was in trouble. As a reward, the stranger told him that he could have three wishes for himself and his descendants. The ancestor wished to be musical, to be fair of face and to have a sense of humour. Because he had not asked for wealth, all three wishes were granted and his descendants were ever blessed with these attributes. On the death of a member of the family, music would be heard in the darkness of night playing around the house. This music was so hauntingly sad that it would reach the innermost parts of the heart. People said that it was fairy music, and that it must have been a fairy who granted those wishes.

Kitty and Larry were champion fiddle players and in later life, when most of Kitty's memories lay dormant in her brain, her musical instincts would sometimes awaken and she and Larry would sit outside their door and give their concert. This was usually in summer, and as the haunting melodies stole across the hills and bogs and fields, people would come out of their houses to listen entranced to this fairy music. Intermingling with the waters of the lakes, the hills and valleys acting as a natural amplifier, this magical sound would reach our ears and add balm to our souls. It was truly God's concert and one of the most treasured memories I have. Whenever I hear a fiddle being played I remember these two people long gone from this earth, and that haunting music comes streaming back across the years, reminding me of those happy childhood days when we were allowed to wander at will among the villages.

Kitty and Larry had relatives in the area but they seldom visited, and some of the immediate family had gone to seek their fortunes elsewhere. There was one sister, Liza, who was working in a big house somewhere in another county. She never married and would return every year for a holiday. Liza was rather grand in speech and dress. She was the topic of conversation while she was in the village and long after she had gone. We would have great fun trying to talk posh like her.

She would also go for walks accompanied by her pets. In those days it was unusual to see a dog on a lead, but it was more unusual to see a *bainbh* or young pig on a lead. It seems that the runt of a litter born on the farm while Liza was in residence was adopted by her and trained to walk with her little dog, 'Master Prim'. The *bainbh* she generally addressed as 'Molly my Sweet'. We would visit the house on any excuse just to watch Liza pamper her pets. We usually ambled in uninvited and plonked ourselves on whatever seat was available. Once I sat on a box by the fire and Liza came from the parlour and screamed blue murder while dragging me off the box. 'Molly my Sweet is in there. You have probably smothered her.' You would imagine I had committed some foul crime as the family rushed from all directions on hearing the commotion. Anyway, all was well. The *bainbh* was fast asleep and order was restored, but I went home shamefaced and was only afterwards able to observe the quaint old lady from a distance.

THE TOFF

NORA KELLY WAS the big toff in our village; or she tried to be. She was always bemoaning the fact that nature had dealt her a severe blow by causing her to be born into a poor family in the heart of the country, when all she hankered after were the bright lights of the city – any city. But nevertheless, here she was, surrounded by a desolate landscape, a victim of circumstance, tied to a small farm that stood in the middle of a bog, with a sickly brother, John, to look after.

A long, winding boreen separated them from the heart of the village and no-one else passed her door as the river Ash flowed from the mountain past her house. No bridge spanned the torrent of water as it raced through the wilderness towards the lake, where it narrowed and, nearing journey's end, relaxed a little, as if its energy was spent. Here the bridge was built that linked the villages and was a meeting-place for the young.

Shops, church and post-office and school all stood around the waterway, but Nora seldom passed this way as she did her shopping in the town. The local shops were not up to her standards, and she tried to impress the shopkeepers in the town with her grandiose ideas. They would be invited to tea at the weekend, or to parties. No such invitation was extended to neighbours unless they were returned exiles or people who had risen to a higher station in life by extra schooling or had served their time to some trade. To her, the poor peasant villagers were rough diamonds, and unless you had a little culture you were excluded from Nora's party list.

Her house was palatial compared with the other habitations in our village, due to the fact that she was able to cajole old men in the area, offering them a home when old age, or some ailment, rendered them incapable of looking after themselves. Usually those unfortunates had no relative to care for them and they would leave home and take up residence with this generous benefactress. She would dance attendance on her paying guests until she gained their gratitude and confidence. Then she would sweet-talk them into signing over their inheritance, lock, stock and barrel. Their pension-books were also an extra inducement, enabling Nora to live the luxury she was getting accustomed to.

As soon as these elderly residents were called from this life Nora put their farms up for sale, acquiring a nice nest-egg for her short investment in someone's life and health. This happened three times over a period of ten years, and woe betide any long-lost relative of any of her guests who turned up looking for a will. They got a cold reception because Nora always had her business legally transacted. A will was contested at one stage and accusations made, but Nora won her case. She was a formidable foe and sued for defamation of character. She also won this case and was awarded damages.

Nora headed for the big city, Dublin, on a giant spending spree. The gossipers were working overtime. All kinds of speculations were made as to what she would be doing in Dublin. In two weeks she was back, dressed to kill and heavily made-up with fingernails as red as blood. We stood at the gable of our house as she passed in a hire-car, trying to catch a glimpse of this Delilah. John, her brother, had the latest records and 'His master's voice' would ring over the bogs for days until he got tired of winding his gramophone. There were new curtains for the parlour and some other new objects and ornaments to add to this already luxurious room in this isolated, slated house, in the bog on the edge of nowhere.

Nora did not believe in dirtying her hands if she could help it, but she got her work done. She had great ingenuity. She would rely on the old custom of the *meitheal*. She would ask all the able-bodied men and women, usually the younger ones (some would come without any invitation), to give one or two days' work without any monetary reward. The porter would flow like buttermilk on these occasions and there would be plenty of food. Delicacies that were strangers to country tables were an added enticement.

Old faithfuls, custards and jellies, would be cooling on the outside windowsills for days beforehand, and spicy currant-cakes sent their aroma out through the windows to where we children would be minding the cows, as only a stream divided our strip of grazing common-land from Nora's. So we would make excuses to go to the house on the pretext of being thirsty, hoping we would be offered some tasty morsel. We were often disappointed as Nora had no great time for children. John was more generous towards us and would sneak some raisins or orange and lemon peel which was coated with sugar, and this we relished as it was only a Christmas delicacy in our own home.

Following the hard day's work at Nora's, which was also a day of laughter and merriment, the people would return to their own homes, get washed and put on their best clothes and head back for Nora's hooley. The fiddlers and anyone who could knock a tune out of any instrument would be invited to provide music for this occasion. Then the big kitchen floor would resound to the stamp of men's boots, as they whirled their part-ners in gay abandonment to the familiar tunes of haunting Irish melodies handed down through the ages.

In between the dances there would be story-telling, step-dancing and joke-telling. The parlour would be used for eating only. This was Nora's sanctum and she watched over the room and supervised the helpers whom she engaged for that night. A certain etiquette and decorum had to be observed, and anyone who misbehaved in Nora's parlour was severely reprimanded.

The dining table seated about twelve people so the banquet went on for hours. The lights from all the rooms shone out like beacons over the moors, and all the youngsters in the village who were not old enough to participate in these hooleys would stand on the fences and look towards the house of merriment. The music reached our ears, taunting us with longings to be grown-up, when we could enjoy the event which was slowly dying out. At dawn the revellers would wearily make their way home, eagerly anticipating another such occasion when they could enjoy work and pleasure in a way which, to country people, was so socially acceptable.

Thus Nora and John had their crops safely harvested by the *meitheal* and also the turf, which was in plentiful supply, practically on their door-steps. When dry, it was usually brought home and stacked by one of the village lads, who was glad of the extra few shillings paid by Nora.

Once a year the hire-car would arrive to take John to town. Nora would accompany him on this annual excursion as he was not a worldly wise man and would probably be taken advantage of in the shops. With his sister in tow, all purchases would be vetoed, but John would manage to buy us a bag of sweets and drop them outside our house on his way home. This was done unknown to Nora as she sat up in the front of the car with its driver. Naturally, we would be lined up at the gable of our house as soon as we heard the car in the distance, and we would dive for the sweets and divide the spoils when the trio were safely out of view.

Their dog, Keeper, had to mind the house while his masters were away. Everyone for miles around had to listen to the dog's lamentations as he cried piteously all day long for the two people he loved, whom he thought had abandoned him. He would sit on the old, disused lime-kiln and it was heartbreaking having to listen to his wailing. No amount of coaxing would entice him from his vigil, and food offered would be left untouched, until at dusk, the sound of the car would reach his ears and he would race to the end of the boreen to meet them. John would get out and man and dog would walk the rest of the way home, happy in each other's company.

As the years passed John's eyesight failed a little so Nora decided he should apply for the blind pension. The forms were duly signed and sent to the appropriate offices. The pension officer must have made a few discreet enquiries on his rounds and the rumours he heard warranted further investigation. Eye specialists were sent to examine John's eyes, but he sat in the corner tapping his stick while the specialist tried to trap him by various means. John had been well-versed by his sister, so he pretended he was deaf also.

A few visits were made by the pension officer trying to catch the malingerer out, but the dog gave the warning that a stranger was on the way. John would put his dark glasses on and take his seat by the fire. Eventually everyone became suspect: the hen-buyer, the herring-seller and the feather-buyer. These hucksters were no longer allowed access to the house as Keeper was set on them, and he could be vicious when ordered.

The applications were persistently sent by Nora until the pension was eventually granted, to the amazement of the locals, who saw John attending regularly to the domestic affairs without his tapping stick. Nora had once more added another source of income to her coffers. It gave people something to talk about for a long time but John, much to his annoyance, had to wear the dark glasses when Nora entertained her friends from the town.

John eventually died of old age. Now Nora was free, she advertised her farm in overseas papers and described her property so eloquently that she found a buyer who purchased it without viewing, at an inflated price, of course. To the amazement of the villagers Nora had once again acquired a sizeable sum of money, which enabled her to spend her remaining years in comfort. She ended her days at a seaside resort in a little hotel overlooking the sea, a lady of leisure as she always wanted to be, still trying to impress and win wealthy and influential friends.

CHAPTER 16

GREAT-UNCLE HAMISH

HAMISH DURKIN WAS my father's uncle and lived in the village of Boyhalla near Slieverue, with the Ox Mountains looming over the hills, valleys and bogs like a giant protector. He was once tall and sandy-haired and in his old age still boasted about his full head of hair. His moustache was grey, but speckled brown under his nose as he used to take snuff. He carried his snuff box in his waistcoat pocket and when we went to visit we would coax a pinch of snuff. We would experiment with this, never realizing it was powdered tobacco. It would burn our noses and my mother would say, 'Serves ye right. Ye can't wait to be grown up,' and she would send us out to the barrel of rain-water to wash our noses out.

Hamish was a bachelor and walked with the aid of a stick. He was slightly bent and after a hard day's work on the farm had to cook and do the household chores, as there was no woman in the house since his mother's death. We would ask why he never married, and with a gleam in his eye he would say there were so many girls chasing after him that he could not decide which one to wed, so they went off and married someone else.

My father's brother, Martin, was promised the farm on condition that he left his home and came to look after Hamish, which he did on a part-time basis for a while. Uncle Martin was in the full bloom of youth: tall and dark-haired, with sloe-black eyes that twinkled with laughter. He was never short of a girl-friend and could have his pick of any of the eligible maidens in the area. But, alas, Hamish insisted on a dowry. Money was scarce and Uncle Martin was in a hurry to own the farm which now had an added incentive; a brand-new slated house with a scullery, which the local, humble thatched cottages lacked.

A widow who was their immediate neighbour had a daughter, Bea, in America. Her fervent wish was that her only daughter would come back and marry locally. The mother's letters across the water were full of praise for this young, hand-some man who was to inherit the Durkin farm, and invitations for Bea to come on holiday and see for herself. This Bea duly did and as soon as Uncle Martin set eyes on the lovely lassie with the lithesome figure and flame-red hair reaching to her waist he fell head over heels in love. Bea was completely smitten by the ardour of this young man's courtship, and the shores of

America were forgotten in her new-found happiness. Bea also happened to be in possession of that most sought after placator 'the dowry', so Hamish gave his consent, and Martin and Bea were wed, with the farm signed over to the happy couple. This was my first memory of a wedding, and I can recall the newly-weds coming to visit us shortly after the ceremony. We thought Bea was a real Yank with her posh clothes and American accent.

As the pair settled down to married life we did not see them very much except for mass on Sundays, as they lived about three miles away. Uncle Martin used to spend some months away in England working for the farmers. Gangs of men used to leave their home every year, including my own father and brothers. The women were left to look after the children and work the farms as best they could.

Bea asked my mother at mass one Sunday if she would spare me for two weeks to look after the baby while she tried to save the turf (dry and stack the turf which had already been cut by her husband). The following Sunday I had to say goodbye to my mother and go with Bea from mass. I was heart-broken. I was only ten and this was the first time I was away from the bosom of my family. I helped as best I could with the household chores and looked after my little cousin. I also had to help with the turf and the weather was not very favourable. We would leave the baby in a *cisean*, or wicker basket, in some sheltered spot while we did constant battle with the elements and the bog, trying to wrest the precious fungi from the marsh.

Bare feet were much in evidence – shoes were a hindrance on the bog as they would be lost in the spongy wet ground. Most times we were forced to carry the sods of turf to higher ground to dry, using a handbarrow. Our legs and hands were stained brown from constant contact with the peat bogs. We would wash in the stream coming home in the evening. The days were so long and I was so homesick. I used to climb the hill overlooking the house every evening, from where I could see my own home away in the distance. I would cry my fill and pray that my mother would come and take me home, but I was promised for two weeks. It was an eternity to me.

I was not getting much sleep either as there was a disturbance in my bedroom. I can remember vividly the constant rattle under the bed, something forever rolling up and down. As the only furniture in the room was a single iron bed I used to wonder why I could not see anything. I was longing for Sunday as I would see my mother at mass. My pale face and red-rimmed eyes told their own story. My mother asked me if I was sleeping well. I said I was in and out of bed all night trying to find what was making the noise under my bed. She said to my uncle's wife, 'Don't tell me you put her in that room? Sure that's never been used since the house was built. Even the dog won't venture in there. May God forgive you, Bea, for putting my child in such danger. And old Hamish himself, why did he allow it? Well, from now on, not one of my kids will ever darken your door again.' And so she grabbed my hand and set off down the road with me in tow, leaving Bea dumbfounded outside the church gates.

I was delighted to be going home, and the room was never mentioned in my presence again. Years afterwards I was told that the room was haunted. No one could explain why this part of the house was inhabited by something that was determined to have this space for itself. The room was sealed afterwards and I never set foot in that house again. I was also told that a few years previously, the body of a young girl had been found by a family cutting turf in the same area of bog where I was helping. The body was perfectly preserved, even to the colour of her hair. Her age was estimated to be about nineteen. People came from far and wide to see this apparition that had lain in the boggy grave for God knows how long.

The people speculated as to who she might be and why, at this moment in time, the bog gave up its gruesome secret. Did it receive the young girl's body by accident or was it an accessory and as compensation preserved the body from the ravages of time? Was it foul murder or had she accidently strayed into the bog in a storm?

In living memory no-one had gone missing. The oldest inhabitants had come to look on the face, but did not recognize her, or if they did, they denied this knowledge. Maybe she was a servant who had crossed the mountain going to take up her post in the town or one of the gentry's houses, and had gone astray. People said that she had come back as a silent accuser and the guilty one, if still alive, would know no peace of mind from then on. The discovery got wide publicity, but no-one came forward to claim the body. Masses were offered for the repose of her soul, and whenever stories were told around the fire the girl in the bog was not forgotten.

CHAPTER 17

THE
BRIDEOGS

T HE FIRST OF February, St Brigid's Day, or *Le Feile Bridha*, Brigid's Feast Day as it was properly known, was welcomed by everyone, especially in agricultural areas. It denoted the first day of spring and the beginning of the farming year. This saint was also known as Brigid of the Dairy and stories vary as to her birth. One legend says she was born into a noble family and as a young maiden was greatly sought after in marriage as her virtues were many. Her father promised her to a landed gentleman but Brigid had already given her heart to God. She refused to marry the man chosen, so as punishment for her disobedience, her father banished her from her apartments, where she had maids to wait on her and obey her every wish, to the dairymaid's quarters. She had to work with them in the dairy, milking and churning and scrubbing and cleaning, until her soft hands were raw and her feet bled with the constant cold. But she suffered these hardships, offering them to God, and still refused her father's demands to marry.

She had a generous heart and the poor used to come begging to her dairy, and she never sent them away empty-handed. Although there was a constant stream of beggars asking to be fed, and Brigid was seemingly giving away all her father's food, yet her stocks never seemed depleted.

Her father marvelled at this, and as he was not a Christian, realised that the God his daughter worshipped must, indeed, be the True One. He was converted and legend says that he was baptised by St Patrick himself, and Brigid was allowed to dedicate her life to helping others.

Another legend says that she once asked a nobleman in the area for land to build an alms-house. He mockingly told her to lay her cloak on the ground and she could have that space to build. She did as he requested and her cloak started to spread until a vast area of land was covered. As the nobleman witnessed this miracle he begged her forgiveness for mocking her piety and her God and willingly granted her the land.

Through her charitable works and holiness her fame spread throughout Christian Ireland. Everyone made crosses on the eve of her feast, dipped them in Holy Water and hung them over the doors and over beds. People would also put them in cow-byres, and man and beast were guarded from fire, weather, injury and disease by invoking the protection of this holy woman.

The crosses were made from rushes which were always pulled, not cut. They had to be woven from left to right, and as we plaited the freshly pulled rushes, the frothy sap would run down our chins and onto our clothes. We became quite skilled at plaiting them and had competitions as to how many we could do and how long it took. We would practise for weeks beforehand and spend hours searching out the best clump of this spongy, green plant. It had to be the best to honour our saint.

On the Eve of St Brigid, 'Brideog's Night', the young men and women of the parish would dress up in anything that would conceal their true identity, wearing face masks and straw hats. An effigy of the saint would be carried, whittled from wood or made of straw. This was called 'The Brideog'. Anyone who could play a musical instrument would bring it along, and as the Brideogers made their way from house to house, dancing and singing, they would be rewarded with something to eat or drink; perhaps even with money if they were lucky.

It was the custom in some areas that one of the Brideogs wore a straw rope with crosses attached, and it was believed that if one of those were passed under a person it prevented illness. This rope was called Brigid's Girdle. There was also the quaint but lovely custom of tying a ribbon outside the house. It was known as *Ribin Breege* or Brigid's Ribbon. If the saint on her feast day happened to be wandering around, it was hoped she would touch the ribbon and endow it with healing powers. Thus it would be treasured and hung around her picture or statue. Refreshments were also left out in case the good saint wanted something to eat, and a bundle of straw to rest her weary bones. Devotion to Brigid formed a daily part of people's lives. Any girl child born on or around this time was bestowed with her name and was expected to follow her good example.

When the Brideogers came home in the early hours of the morning, tired and weary from celebrating the eve of the saint's feast, they would gently lift the latch of their doors so as not to disturb her in case she had taken refuge for the night under their roofs.

The first snows on the mountains were known as the white-cloak of Brigid, and the first flowers of spring were placed before her statue. She was also known as Mary of the Gael. She is buried in County Down, and shares the same tomb as St Patrick and St Colmeille. 'Three Saints one grave do fill: St Patrick, Brigid and Colmeille.' She was originally buried in Kildare where she was born, but her coffin was removed to County Down for safety during the Danish invasion, as the Danes plundered graves for valuables and often stole the coffin itself, depending on what it was made from.

CHAPTER 18

LENT AND
ST PATRICK'S DAY

LENT WAS STRICTLY observed in our home, especially by the grown-ups. It was black fast for them on Ash Wednesday and every Friday during Lent, especially Good Friday – tea without sugar or milk and dry bread. All the children who had reached the use of reason, which was generally supposed to be the age of seven years, were expected to give up something: sweets, sugar, jam, or maybe cocoa. The pledgings would be made, but some did not last twenty-four hours.

Shrove Tuesday was also known as Mardi Gras, or Fat Tuesday, as people feasted on that day. Before the fast began, pancakes would be made to use up eggs, milk, and flour. During Lent, oaten bread would be eaten. It was a traditional time for weddings, as marriage was forbidden during Lent. If couples did not marry at Shrovetide it was taken for granted that they would not marry for another year.

The Sunday after Shrove Tuesday was known as Chalk Sunday. People of marriageable age who remained single had a chalk mark made on their backs. Sometimes their age was chalked instead, much to the embarrassment of the young men or women concerned, but it was a bit of fun for the youngsters in the area.

Butchers could not sell meat during Lent so herrings were the order of the day. They were cheap and nourishing but by the end of six weeks, the sight and smell of fish would make people sick. There was a custom in certain parts of Ireland of 'burying the herring' at the end of Lent. A large fish was selected and carried around until a suitable resting-place was found, when it was buried ceremoniously and joyously by all the people.

On Ash Wednesday everyone went to church for the ashes. Some brought their own turf ash, or ash from the blessed palms from the year before. We were reminded by the priest as he put the sign of the cross on our foreheads with the holy ashes, that we were but mere mortals, and he would say to each person, 'Remember, man, that thou art but dust, and into dust thou shalt return.' We would wear this sign with the greatest reverence and would not dare wash our foreheads in case we touched the holy oils mixed with ash. We did not deem ourselves worthy of doing so.

There was one day in Lent that gave people a break from the harsh religious observances, and that was St Patrick's Day. It was like a beacon shining out of the darkness. Even in the strictest times meat was allowed on this day, and those who were abstaining from the 'gargle' (poteen) were allowed to drown the shamrock. In times gone by, after the main meal of the day, the shamrock was placed in a glass of punch. A toast was drunk to the good saint, then the shamrock was removed from the glass and thrown over the left shoulder. This was also considered a lucky day to plant potatoes and was considered the first day of spring sowing. Once St Patrick's Cross used to be worn instead of a shamrock. These were made from white paper and different in design for men and women.

Another custom was the blessing of horses. As the plougher worked his team they were turned in the direction of the sun at the end of each furrow. The sower would bless the work in the name of the Trinity and toss a handful of the newly turned earth over each horse.

This day of celebration over, we looked forward to Palm Sunday and Easter Sunday. Palm Sunday was commemorated by the blessing of the palms and each family took one home to take its place of honour behind a holy picture, there to remind us of the triumphant entry into Jerusalem of Jesus on the donkey, when people waved palm branches and strewed the ground with a carpet of palms in his honour.

Maundy Thursday was the first day of Easter. The houses were spring cleaned and bunches of wild flowers were picked to adorn the house. On this holy Thursday people generally walked to church for the re-enactment of the Last Supper, and the Maundy ceremony of the washing of the feet. Then the Blessed Sacrament would be taken from the tabernacle to the Altar of Repose, and the door of the Holy of Holies left wide open until Easter Sunday. The church would be in mourning with the crucifixes and statues draped in purple.

On Good Friday we would go to the church again to participate in the age-old ceremonies of the Stations of the Cross and the kissing of the cross. On Holy Saturday the church would still be in mourning and then would dawn Easter Sunday. We would be up to see the sun dance with joy as it did on that first Easter Sunday at the resurrection of the Saviour. It was a joyous day also as the fasting was over.

At breakfast we were allowed as many eggs as we could eat. In those days eggs were a luxury as they were usually sold or bartered for essentials for the household. We always had some new item of clothing for good luck to wear to mass on this day. The dinner was a feast and lamb was eaten in commemoration of the paschal lamb. A big dance would be held on Easter Sunday night and if you were coming of age this was the night to be initiated into the world of grown-ups. You would go to your first dance.

People made the most of these landmarks in our calendar and they helped sustain a community spirit. Dances were not allowed during Lent, and the pastors of the flock preached fervently against company-keeping in this penitential time. There was the odd one who broke the rule and the priest always got to know. He would publicly rebuke those wrong-doers from the pulpit after Lent, not naming names of course, but the blushes were brought to the cheeks of the guilty and it was another topic of conversation on the way home from mass.

Children had their own fun. In some parts of the country they would go *cludoging* or collecting eggs from neighbours who kept hens. Egg-rolling was once a popular game. Also Christians adopted the egg as the symbol of the resurrection. In olden times the egg was considered a thing of mystery, seemingly dead, with life within. Eventually chocolate eggs were substituted for the real thing. In medieval times eggs were brought to church. At antiphon, bishops and priests would dance and throw the eggs at the choristers, who would pass them from one to the other as the dancing and singing continued.

Special spicy bread was baked for Easter with a cross marked in it. If a loaf baked at this time was kept, it was thought to ensure protection for the year and if part of the bread was rubbed on sores it had healing properties. Long ago small spiced cakes used to be put in the coffins of the dead, but these old customs are long-since gone.

CHAPTER 19

THE
NEIGHBOURS

P EOPLE WHO LIVED in our small farming community must have thought that my mother produced her offspring as a source of continuous cheap labour for their benefit. We were the largest family in the area, so requests for our help were always coming in, especially at school holiday time.

In spring, when the fields were ploughed and harrowed and made ready for the usual crops to be sown – wheat, corn and barley – our first job would be to replenish the *mala mors*, or big bags, which the sower wore around his waist with the appropriate seeds. The bags of seed would be filled from the large barrels of grain kept in the granary and brought to a convenient spot by the headland in the field where the fresh soil was waiting to receive and nurture it.

It was a joyful sight; a biblical scene. Man sowing the seed, throwing hope into the air, hoping that when it fell, that the

God-given earth and a combination of the elements would yield a good harvest in due course. Harrowing would again be repeated to cover the seed and then the back-breaking task of picking the stones would begin: stones which the plough and harrow had unearthed from their slumbering where they had lain for centuries. These would be collected and added to the dry-stone walls which marked the boundaries between fields.

The *Fear Breaga* or False Man, would then be made, and with due pomp and ceremony he would be placed in the middle of the field to keep his vigil frightening the birds. We would change his location from time to time, hoping to deceive the cunning crows. They would eventually realize he was harmless and mockingly post their own sentries on his outstretched arms while their friends feasted on our grain. When the birds became too daring, a blast from the shotgun would provide victims to hang on the *Fear Breaga*. The crows would then sit on the fences screaming vengeance at the perpetrators of such an abominable act, and that scene would be repeated throughout the villages until the fields put on the mantle of green, giving hope for the future harvest and rewards for man's labour.

In the meantime, the splitting of the potatoes would begin. This was a specialist job: being able to recognize the growing potential of each potato and separating and cutting the eyes – these were called slits – to be sown for the future crop. The *seelawns*, the discarded part, would be boiled and fed to the fowl and pigs. All the younger members of the family had to pitch the potatoes and would follow the person boring the holes with a *stieven*. This was a long piece of wood narrowing to a point, which was covered in a circle of iron. There was a cleft in the wood so that pressure would be added by foot to make the hole, and we would drop a slit into each hole, covering the precious seed with soil before nightfall.

In the weeks and months that followed, farmyard manure would be spread on the ridges, and fresh soil dug and added to nurture the growing stalks now visible. Then the planting would be done by a second addition of soil, but this time the soil would be firmly tapped into place with the back of the spade to give stability to the now half-grown potato stalk. Then came more fertilizer and eventually the spraying.

The water had to be brought from the river and the barrels filled. Blue stone would be added and testings taken with a special paper dipped in the barrel. When the paper showed a specific colour it was ready for use. The machine would be filled, strapped to the sprayer's back and spraying would begin, protecting the crop against blight. This was repeated three times and was a back-breaking job. The contraption often leaked and as the sprayer laboriously worked his way in the *shoecks*, or trenches, up and down between the ridges he was soaked to the skin. He was eventually rewarded with the magnificent sight of the potato fields covered in yellow or white blossom.

When the sun and rain had co-operated with nature the results were worth the hard labour. Our own work was hardly over before the people who needed help were at our door asking my mother for the loan of one of her children. They would say, 'Mary, can you spare one or two of the kids?', and of course, she would not refuse but would say, 'Indeed you're welcome to them any time.' We had our favourites who would already have bribed us with the promise to teach us a song or tell us a story. A man by the name of Padriac Conlon had more songs than any of our temporary masters and we would be at his house bright and early.

I associate certain fields in the village with songs I learned in those wonderful innocent days of childhood, particularly 'Paddy McGinty's Goat' and 'Father Tom O'Neill'. There were thirty-two verses to be learned and we were willing pupils. We would then tell them to the other members of our family. Padriac would say to us each evening, 'Now if you don't come tomorrow, then you won't have the end of the song, or the rhubarb pie,' which his wife, Peggy, always made especially for us as an added inducement. She would send me home laden with great sticks of rhubarb and would warn me against giving any away, especially to a neighbour they were not on speaking terms with. This neighbour we liked so she got her share without anyone being aware of the deceit.

We hated going to Roger Fada's (Long Roger's) house as he

was a slave-driver and we would cry and beg our mother not to send us. My grandfather would say, 'Mary, why are you sending them to that long string of misery, he will knock the last drop of sweat out of them and starve them into the bargain. Send something to eat with them.' My mother would say, 'Shaun, I can't shame myself doing that. What would they think?' We would get something to eat brought to the field in case we wasted too much time indoors. Roger would sit on the fence during the day gossiping with anyone passing by, extolling our virtues to one and all while we worked like hatters. After a hard day's work we had to walk a long distance home, glad to see the back of that village. We would complain about how hard we worked but my soft-hearted mother would say, 'Now if ye did not help, his poor wife Katie, who's not in the best of health would have to be in the fields.' That would console us a little as Katie was as kind as her husband was mean.

Preparations were now being made for the cutting of the turf and this was keenly anticipated by the older brothers and sisters who were fancy free. The time would be arranged weeks beforehand at the local dances, and on a given day all the lads and lassies would come down from the hills and across the dells. Anyone without a bicycle would take the short cuts through the fields and follow the paths by the streams and rivers, all heading for the bog which was a couple of miles away. They would call good-naturedly to each other as they met, and looked forward to the fun as well as the hard work. It was a social gathering also as they would come together to eat their homemade soda bread and eggs. The bottles of milk would be buried in a bog-hole to keep them cool, and the spring water for the tea and the quenching of the thirst would be brought from the nearest well and left between the cold, wet sods of turf taken from the spongy marsh where it had been nurtured for centuries. The fires would be lit for boiling the water and eggs, and the taste of tea made on the bog was unequalled. The smoke from the myriads of fires rising as from miniature wigwams wafted in the breeze and lingered long after the flames had burnt out.

The turf-cutter used a slane, a type of long-handled spade, and neighbours would compete with each other as to the amount cut each day. Each cutter had to have a person to catch each sod as he expertly enticed it from its place of birth. The spreader would be equally expert at receiving the pulpy piece of black fungi and throwing it, without breaking it, into the surrounding heather to dry. It was another back-breaking job but a necessary and important task for the well-being of the families involved.

The turf would be left to dry for days or weeks according to the weather, then it would be reckeled – small amounts standing at angles to let the wind through. Then it would be clamped – larger amounts built into small stacks and left for the sun and wind to finish the process. Eventually it would be brought to the road ready for its final journey to be stacked beside the house for winter.

The drawing of the turf was a joyful time, but not for us youngsters. We had to help fill the carts while our older brother or sister would set off on the homeward journey sitting contentedly on top of the load. We would be barrowing out late cuts of turf if the bog was wet. We had to use a hand-barrow, with one in front and one at the back. Many a time the kesh, or temporary bridge, collapsed and barrow, turf and children ended up in the bog-hole to be rescued by some neighbour who chided us for carrying the lazy man's load, overloading to get the job finished more quickly. The braying of asses could be heard for miles, and many a jackass who would not normally pull a cart would do so willingly so as to make the acquaintance of some female donkey.

As the bog was quite a distance from our house, three cartloads were the most that could be managed in one day. It took six weeks to draw enough to last the winter. The general topic of conversation at this time was who had the biggest and best-made stack. It was a very competitive time but very rewarding. The sight of all the winter's fuel beside each house added an extra glow to the humble homesteads of our thriving little village of long ago.

CHAPTER 20

THE
THRESHING

HEN THE CHUGGING sound of the threshing machine could be heard at work in the distance, it was the signal for the start of feverish activity around most farmhouses. Cartways and pathways had to be cleared; branches of trees and small bushes cut and strewn over the soft ground to form a solid basis for the machine in case it bogged down. Bags for grain had to be gathered together, washed in the river and holes repaired – coming along any country road around threshing time it was not unusual to see bags drying on walls, stacks of turf and on bushes. The packing needles and twine would be got ready to sew the newly filled bags of grain and everyone had their own job to do.

Our excitement would reach fever-pitch as the sound of the thresher got nearer and as this monster, with smoke belching from its funnel, came into sight of our village, the younger

THE THRESHING

members of our family would be waiting to escort it into our haggard. The men and women of the neighbourhood would leave their own work and come and give a hand with their hayforks balanced on their shoulders with corks on the prongs in case of accident. The dogs would also accompany their masters, sure of fun and games galore with the rats who had made their homes in the stacks. The men with the *sugans,* or straw ropes, tied round their trouser bottoms to stop the rats seeking refuge where they shouldn't, hoisted the sheaves to the men kneeling on the machine platforms. They in turn fed the sheaves into the gaping, greedy mouth of this quivering mass of steel. More men were filling and removing the bags of grain that came speeding down the shoots, while the women sewed the mouths of the bags with twine. These were eventually carried to the granary.

More sturdy workers cocked or ricked the straw, which would be used as fodder for the animals in the winter months. If it was windy the chaff would blow all over: up your nose, in your hair and on your clothes. It was like bedlam in the haggard with the noise from the engine, the people shouting at each other above the din, children shrieking and running hither and thither, trying to evade the rats and mice who had been evicted from their homes. The dogs barked and yelped with murder in their hearts as they chased these demented rodents to a sudden end.

At dusk, all would make for the house, where the women

were busy getting supper, ravenous with hunger. Mugs of porter would be handed around to allay the big thirst and to wet the whistle as the wits of the party would say. Chickens and hams would be cooked; the lovely smell of home-made spicy currant-bread titillating the palate while we eagerly awaited our turn to eat. On occasions like this we would be looking forward to the apple and blackberry tarts, and many other delicacies which were not everyday fare in country homes. The big kitchen table would be brought to the middle of the floor, and everyone would eat and drink their fill. The big black kettle would be hung on the crook over the turf fire to refill the equally big enamel teapot that nestled on the coals by the fire, and laughter and cheerful banter would resound around the kitchen until people got tired.

When the threshing machine moved on to the next farm, so the helpers followed, lending a hand there, as was the custom. When the grain was safe in the granaries, some to be kept for use for animals and fowl, some to be kept for seed for the next year's sowing and some brought to the mill to be ground, a certain amount of grain would be retained by the miller in exchange for the grinding. Money would also be accepted as payment but money was scarce.

The threshing-parties would then begin and music and dancing would go on in certain houses until the early hours. People celebrated the harvest festival their own way. In olden times the church was the centre of celebrations. The host was made from the first wheat to be harvested and milled at Lammas (Loaf Mass). Everyone gathered to celebrate mass and to ask God's blessing for the work that lay ahead. This was August the first, and Michaelmas was September the twentieth. The feast of Michael the Archangel marked the end of the harvest, when there were thanksgiving prayers and feasting.

In pagan times, the earth was supposed to be a goddess who had to be placated, if she rendered a good harvest, with the blood of a young man. The man who felled the last sheaf was killed by his workmates so that his blood could soak into the soil. With the coming of Christianity the gruesome sacrifice was discontinued, and a tradition still lingers in some areas whereby the last sheaf is left standing. Hence, the saying, 'the grim reaper' and the ghosts of the dead murdered in ignorance and superstition carrying their scythes are still told of in folklore. So God took the place of those fearsome goddesses, and harvest masses and thanksgiving were rendered to him instead.

Some farmers did their threshing the old way with the flail. This was a staff with a short, heavy stick swinging at the end. The swivel joints were made from cow-hide and straw rope. This was a slow process and needed strong arms. First, a wide sheet made from canvas was laid under the sheaves, then the thresher would swing the flail rhythmically around his head and down onto the grain. This went on until the grain was loosed. The chaff mingled with the grain and had to be winnowed later on a windy day. The straw had to be collected and made into bundles to be fed to the cattle. This was also a time for youngsters to learn how to make *sugans*, or straw ropes.

There were also isolated farms which the threshing machine was unable to reach, and we willingly helped when requested. We would replace the sheaves as the flailer finished each one, and we would collect the grain and put it into barrels or bags. The hens had to be shooed away because too much grain made them egg-bound.

We were thankful when the threshing machine finally put an end to the flail in our own home, but for years my grandfather would still keep some sheaves in the barn and the old flail would be taken down from the rafters for old-times' sake, and he would spend happy hours threshing the old-fashioned way and teaching us how to make *sugans*.

CHAPTER 21

TOPSY
AND POLLY

O NE OF THE chores the younger members of our family had to do was to help bring home the cows at milking time. This was a scene familiar in any country area at evening time. To the uninitiated this seems a picture worthy of a story-book: cows ambling along chewing the cud, heedless of anything sharing the highway, and nudging each other for space. It seems so peaceful and serene, part and parcel of any country-side, with man and dog leisurely in attendance.

We children knew differently from bitter experience: it depended on the mood of the cows and no two cows are the same in temperament. Ours was a small farm. We depended on con-acre – leasing neighbour's land – for tilling and grazing. It was usually some distance from our house, so our cows resented the long walk home.

Topsy was our lead cow. We would call her name when we

got within hearing distance and she would answer, lowing several times. She would be waiting patiently by the gate with the other members of the herd gathered about her, their breath smelling sweetly of clovered grass and heather, eager to be home and milked.

The cows always followed the same path, leaving little streams of milk as their udders would be overflowing. The old people used to say that the roads of Ireland were made from the old cow-paths. There was an old saying: 'Where the old cow led, we all follow.' For the younger members of the herd it was play-time. They would take every path but the right one and wander into every open gap to sample the neighbour's grass. Herds in other fields would come to the gates to enjoy the show and give their encouragement with their continuous lowing. Coming to the crossroads they would scatter in all directions as if threatening to leave home.

We would eventually gather them together and get them safely to their byres: milk cows on one side chained to their respective stalls, youngsters on the other side or in separate barns. Pails and buckets would be brought and milking would begin. Mouser, our cat, would sit patiently waiting for his warm supper. He had learned to open his mouth and get a stream of milk straight from the cow's teats. Sometimes several jets of milk would be directed towards Mouser and he would stand on his hind legs and dance around trying to catch the sprays. My brothers and I would roar with laughter at his antics. His hunger temporarily satisfied, he would then scramble up into the loft over the cows and go to sleep in the hay and out of the way of Polly, our cross cow, who would lash out with her hind leg and send Mouser flying when he strayed too near.

Polly was bought at a fair: a bargain so my father said, never realising she had been sold because of her evil ways. This black demon had a flaw in her character that was to terrorize our family and village children and nearly led to tragedy.

Polly had to be double-tied in her stall and fettered at milking times as milk and milker often ended up in the channel covered in cow-dung, with Polly watching with a mean look in her eye, admiring her handiwork. She hated children and although we would dare her, we only did it when we knew we could make a hasty retreat. She would paw the ground, lower her head and charge. We would be over the ditch, out of harm's way, quick as lightning. Constant contact with stone ditches had left Polly with permanent bumps on her forehead, and she bellowed like a bull. She must have had Spanish ancestors, and somewhere in the recesses of her mind the bull-ring called.

One evening as she was being driven home for milking, she broke away from the herd. My little brother was sitting by the gable of the house, and Polly spotted him. He tried to make for the safety of the kitchen door but the treacherous animal saw her chance and attacked the defenceless child. She rolled him around like a football, stamped on him, butted him against the gable and began to bite his legs before he was rescued. Polly had tasted blood and her fate was sealed. Within a few days she was collected to be put down although it was a great loss financially. She could never be trusted as she had murder in her heart. Her notoriety had spread around the villages but we shed no tears for her.

Topsy was the complete opposite of Polly in temperament. In the bovine world she would be considered a beauty. Her colour was amber and with her glossy coat, big, doe-like eyes and gentle disposition she was loved by all the family. I used to imagine her as the 'mythical cow of plenty' from the story told to us by the *Seanchai*, the storyteller. The cow of plenty belonged to 'Gobnue the Smith' and she was supposed to crop the grass so quickly that in a day's grazing she often went from one end of Ireland to the other. She gave as much milk in a day as a whole herd of cows would give in a month. Balor of the evil eye set his heart on this fine animal and sent a man to steal her. The thief came in the dead of night but Gobnue heard him and rose from his bed. The thief got away in the darkness, but the cow's magic halter had gone and Gobnue had to watch his cow morning, noon and night in case she strayed into Balor's country after her halter.

In my innocence I would sit with Topsy, warning her of the evil Balor. Oftentimes she would lick my face with her raspy tongue and it would tingle and hurt, but I did not mind. It was her way of telling me she loved me. I often went to sleep lulled by the warmth in the cow-byre and the rhythm of the munching and chewing of the day's grass, which they regurgitated at their leisure.

When the milking was over the young calves would get their share; there would be so much put aside for general use, and the remainder left to cool. Next day the cream would be skimmed off and put into an earthenware pail. When there was sufficient to churn, butter would be made. This was done by using a dash method: an up and down movement. It was an art in itself and very tiring on the arms. Everyone who was able had to take their turn. Hot and cold water were used at a certain time and we learned by watching. Anyone visiting the house while a churning was in session had to lend a hand.

Churning finished, the butter would be put into a wooden bowl and salt worked in. It was washed several times with spring-water until all the milk was washed out, then it would be rolled and patterned, covered, and set aside for use when needed. Coming in from school it was a glorious sight to see the churnful of fresh buttermilk with the left-over *suilíns*, or eyes, of butter floating on top. We would drink mugfuls of it.

On market days, farmers' wives would take home-made butter to the town to sell, as demand was great. Some cheated by soaking the butter in carrot juice to give it a rich, golden colour. We never had to resort to such underhandedness as ours was naturally so from the lush buttercupped and clovered pastures.

The first three days after a cow calved, the milk would not be used in the usual way. It was too rich, so it was boiled with salt added and was a delicacy to be divided amongst the neighbours, and they in turn would return the compliment. It was called 'beastings' and we would be sent with a can-full to relatives also.

There was always an abundance of milk in our home and the surplus fed to pigs and hens. We were not allowed tea so we had to be content with cocoa: made with milk, of course. It was a treat to get a cup of tea in a neighbour's house, and if they were short of milk we would be sent with a bottle.

CHAPTER 22

TINKERS

T HE TINKERS CAME to our district about twice a year, usually under cover of darkness – if they came in daylight they would meet with strong resistance. The morning would find them firmly encamped on the outskirts of some village, an unwelcome sight, especially for the villagers nearest their camp. Nothing was safe, and householders had to be forever vigilant. The tents would be erected and the usual motley group of animals seen busily feeding on everything in sight, while other animals wandered off in search of grazing along the roads and in neighbouring fields.

The highways and byways were trimmed bare by those hungry beasts. There would be children of all ages running hither and thither, with dogs barking, babies crying, traps and side-cars and carts left with their shafts pointing towards the sky, whilst the men of the tribe hammered and shouted as they set up their temporary homes along the highway.

Some of the women would be busy with their daily chores, cooking on the open fires outside their tents with up-turned boxes serving as chairs. They always chose their camping site near running water, and the women would be observed on their knees washing by the river or stream, while others went on their daily rounds begging from house to house. The hedgerows would be bedecked with an array of garments drying under the open skies. Some women would work their way through the villages carrying their babies on their backs, papoose-style, with their big, woollen shawls wrapped around them. They also wore a special ankle-length skirt, with a patchwork of massive pockets specially made for collecting their booty. They depended on the generosity of the householder and would beg for tea, sugar, flour, butter or anything that could be carried in these pouches. Vegetables they would probably plunder from the farms nearest their camp and many were the pitched battles fought between tinkers and farmers.

Some villages would welcome a visit from the travelling people, as the men were tin-smiths and masters of their craft. Some of the men would carry the tools of their trade on their rounds, and as they came into sight of our village the sun would glint on the rolls of tin which were tied and slung across their shoulders. This would be the advance party as some of the men would find work awaiting them along the route. The older men would have some form of transport. They would make tin mugs and tin cans outside the houses, fix pots and pans and buckets. They would also weld and mend farm implements.

The older women would come into the house first, knocking and opening the half door, saying, 'It's Biddy Mahon, it is.' Then would follow the younger members. We would watch fascinated as these seemingly bottomless pockets swallowed up whatever my mother could spare, as she herself had a big family to feed with little resources. The tinker women would ask for a drink of 'tay' and maybe some buttermilk for himself outside working, and a piece of bread for the kids. She would heap blessings on my mother for her generosity and would fervently beseech good health and full and plenty all our lives. We would have our own brand-new, shining mugs made by Biddy's husband, Owen, and we would over-use them for days until they lost their newness.

These wandering tribes had their own code, strictly adhered to. They divided the areas between the different families and no-one would encroach on another's domain, so that over the years we go to know each individual. We would be informed of any births, deaths, or marriages since their last visit, and my mother would comment on the development of the children and admire the new babies, so they were not really strangers as such.

My father would sometimes scold my mother for being over-generous but she would say that we had a roof over our heads and enough to eat and drink, while they slept by the wayside with no place to call home. She would explain to us that the tinkers were not on the road by choice. They were once owners of houses and land but, through some misfortune, had been thrown out and had to struggle to survive, wandering through the countryside depending on charity, whilst the people who dispossessed them lived in comfort.

Some householders shut the doors in their faces, while others set the dogs on them. In winter these displaced people camped on the bog roads away from houses. At least they were sure of a fire and anyone with reserve stacks of turf had to make constant trips to the bog to keep an eye on their property. We always had reserves for selling in the town in winter and it was a welcome source of income. It was stacked on the bog road for easy access and my father or brothers would sell it by the cart-load. The tinkers would assure my family that they would not pilfer from us as we were hospitable to them on their rounds. They only robbed those who showed them the door or turned the dogs on them.

In the cold weather their favourite expression to passers-by was 'T'was a cold night in the tent, Sir.' We used to pity them. They were a hardy race of people. The women of the Mahon family had beautiful golden wavy hair reaching to their waists, and on the coldest, frostiest morning could be seen washing their tresses in the running water of the stream or river. They never used a towel to dry hair but squeezed the excess water out, tossing their crowning glory in the wind, and letting nature do the rest. They would eventually depart, leaving behind the usual mess to be cleaned away by the villagers and dumped out of harm's way. The villagers would say 'Good riddance', and hope that they chose another location next time round.

CHAPTER 23

THE TRAMP

J OHN NANCY WAS a man of the roads. Nobody knew where he came from or where he was going to. Age never seemed to touch him, at least to us children. He was always old in our eyes as he shuffled along the country roads in his old raggedy clothes caked in mud, dried by the sun and wind and as hard as board. Most times he smelled like the animals he found refuge with in someone's barn. When he was offered a roof by some kindly person he would refuse, saying he preferred lodging with the animals or under some hayrick, or even the hedgerow, rather than sleep on a feather tick – although a bed of straw would be the only mattress intended, as there were often no spare beds.

In his wanderings he picked up all sorts of gossip, and in his many years of tramping he accumulated a wealth of knowledge, good and bad, especially about people's pedigrees. He would gladly release his savoury bits of information to anyone who would provide him with a meal. We would hide when we saw him coming round the rock as he was often used as a threat when we misbehaved or would not go to bed: 'John Nancy can have ye next time he calls to the village.' We would plead for mercy and promise to be good. It was better to be good than tramp the countryside with John Nancy with no family and no place to call home. He always wore a cap, or a semblance of one, over his long, unkempt hair. This grew at random through the many holes that rendered his headwear practically useless, so that it was impossible to differentiate between cap, hair and beard as they all blended together.

John would only call at certain houses, usually the least well off as he said they were the ones who would share what little they had. The better off would set the dog on him, and he would rant and rave and call loudly for all to hear the history of their forebears, awaking skeletons from cupboards where they had been under lock and key for years. He knew everyone's background off by heart, and God help anyone who had to bear the lash of his tongue. I remember him once calling at our school. He hobbled straight in through the classrooms, this walking scarecrow, with feet as black as the ace of spades, as he never wore shoes because he maintained if God had wanted us to wear shoes we would have been born with them.

In his estimation teachers were rich so he came begging for

money, but his pleas fell on deaf ears. The teachers were disgusted with this vagabond who dared to intrude on their own smug little world. Some of the stronger older boys were delegated to escort John Nancy from the school, and he was frogmarched through the classroom. To all the schoolchildren, it was like a circus and we were enjoying it. It was unusual to see the teachers taken off guard, and as he was ejected he was shouting abuse at all and sundry. At least two of the teachers were reminded of their ancestry and it was nothing to boast about. One lady who was past the bloom of youth without being wed and who came from a well-to-do family in a town some miles away, heard a few things about her background that she may have been unaware of, ending up with the words, 'With all the money your father's got, he cannot buy you a man, shure an ould spinster you'll be all your life and no man in his right mind would put a ring on the finger of an ould dried up one like yourself. Look at ye, mutton dressed up as lamb. Oh fine feathers make fine birds, but you're nothing but an ould crow.'

Another teacher was reminded of a grandfather's pedigree and how he got his money. John shouted, 'Shure I wouldn't touch a penny of yours now even if you offered it to me, and remember the saying and teach it well to your scholars, "Ill gotten, ill gone." You will rue the day you threw poor old John Nancy out of the school.'

He was still around when the children came out at home-time, and I remember some of the boys jeering him and calling him names. Then to add insult to injury they started pelting his bare feet with stones. He was whining and begging them to stop, while he tried to stand on one foot and rub the wounds where the stones had found their target. That was the last time I saw John Nancy, and that memory of him has since brought tears to my eyes. I do not recall having pleaded his cause that day, but I hope he has forgiven his tormentors. At the time, we could not wait to get home to relay all we had heard to our parents. It caused a bit of excitement in the villages and raised a few laughs too. We wanted to know if there was any truth in his allegations, but were put off with the words, 'There might be a few grains of truth in his ravings but nobody should pay much heed to poor old John, shure he's only an old tramp.'

CHAPTER 24

COUSIN   JOHN

MY MOTHER'S ONLY cousin, John, emigrated to America as a young man and worked as a miner in Illinois. Born in Newcastle-upon-Tyne, he had lost both his parents as a young child, whereupon he and his younger brother, Larry, were sent to Ireland to their uncle, my maternal grandfather.

They arrived in our little town in the West of Ireland with labels tied with string around their waists, on which their names and destinations were boldly printed. It must have been a heart-breaking journey for the two orphans, but they were made welcome and, as my mother was an only child, they soon settled in and were brought up as one family.

The younger brother died in his teens as the result of an accident, and since my mother was the natural heir to the little farm, and there were no real prospects for John at home, the emigrant ship was the only solution. Passage was paid by another relative.

COUSIN JOHN

John's surname, Groarke, sounded more European than Irish, and he had been advised that an Irish surname would be more advantageous in finding employment in America. So he dropped the first letter, replacing it with an apostrophe O'. He now had a typical Gaelic surname which he kept for the rest of his life, passing it on to his children, a son and daughter.

He did not visit his adopted home again until his retirement. By then a widower, he had been given a golden handshake by the mining company for which he worked, in the form of a trip around the world. He had risen from a humble miner, hewing coal at the face, to colliery manager, but throughout that time, he never forgot the debt he owed to my grandfather. The letters came regularly and usually included dollars. After grandfather's death my mother received a letter every Christmas with enough dollars to buy the usual seasonal fare, and many prayers and blessings would be extended to our cousin John for his benevolence.

I shall never forget the excitement in our home at the news that our relative was coming to visit us. Word spread around the locality that 'the Yank' was returning. There was feverish activity in our house. The inside and outside were whitewashed. Barns and walls that had not felt the stroke of a brush for years were now given a new lease of life. Gates that were rickety were mended and given a coat of paint. The house got a new thatch. Hedges were trimmed.

My mother's greatest worry was that our pigs would not be ready for market before the arrival of our visitor. She thought that the smell from the pigsty might offend the nostrils of our illustrious guest, so they were fattened in haste and swiftly dispatched to the bacon factory.

New items of furniture were also purchased and a mattress bought to replace the old, home-made feather tick. Out went the old press and in its place came a commodious wardrobe reaching the ceiling, with an outside mirror and ample hanging-space for the elegant suits and shirts we felt sure this rich cousin would possess. The poor donkey that pulled the cart which transported this grand piece of furniture from the showroom in town, well, he must have felt like the king of donkeys as he made his way homeward through the villages. People came out of their houses to admire this rare commodity and, as the donkey and cart came in sight of our home, we hastened to escort it on the last lap of its journey.

We had only mantlepiece mirrors previously, so for the very first time we were able to admire ourselves full length and, until the novelty wore off, we spent hours prancing and dancing in front of the mirror.

Eventually, the great day dawned and he was in our midst: this giant of a man with a big, jovial face, a thatch of silver hair, a booming voice and a ready laugh. Neighbours and friends came to welcome him back. There were presents for every child, and our joy knew no bounds as we curried for favour and escorted our cousin everywhere, eager to supply little snippets of information, which he always relished.

On the first morning after his arrival, he climbed up to the fields above our house and was amazed to see the hills that surrounded our village. He had completely forgotten them, and the picture he had carried in his mind for all these years was now shattered. He stood looking at the mountains in the distance which he had remembered, wondering why the hills had stolen from his memory.

He was eager to renew old acquaintances, especially with a former girlfriend. When we learned who this ex-girlfriend was we could not believe our ears. How could this wizened, eccentric little woman ever have been the beauty whom our cousin constantly talked about, recounting to young and old his long past romance with Mamie Hughes.

Now Mamie lived several villages away from us and had married, but her husband was long dead and there were no children. We used to visit friends in that same village and had to pass by her door. That was the highlight of our journey as we hoped to catch a glimpse of this frail, old lady who treated her hens as children, calling them names: Pluckstey, Floss, Amber, Bell. She would scold them for not paying attention, and her favourite saying was that the hens were just like Christians. The flourishing growth of hair on her upper lip was the cause of much mirth to the children of the area, which eventually led to Mamie living a solitary existence, shutting her door when she saw or heard anyone coming. Of course, cousin John went to visit her and they spent happy hours reminiscing and reliving their first, sweet romance.

During his long sojourn with us cousin John constantly impressed upon my mother the importance of education. He was amazed at the lack of books in country homes and vowed that when he returned to the States he would send us plenty of reading material. As he was on his way to Australia after visiting Ireland, he promised to send a card from every port of call, with as much information on that country as the writing space would allow.

These were to be our greatest geography lessons. He was visiting his only daughter in Australia, who had married a mining engineer in the USA and was sent to a sister company down under to lend his expertise. I remember cousin John saying that before he left on his tour, he had to sign a form declaring that he would not divulge any of his company's secrets to his son-in-law.

The trip around the world lasted longer than was planned as in the meantime World War II broke out. When he eventually got back to America cousin John kept his promise and we regularly received our magazines – *Colliers*, *Saturday Evening Post* and the *National Geographic Magazine*, much to the annoyance of our local postman as they added extra weight to his already heavy postbag.

COUSIN JOHN

An older brother always censored all reading material before it was passed on to us and deleted whatever he thought offensive. This made us all the more anxious to discover what we had missed. We would try to bribe one of our brothers or sisters to tell us the excised bits and received exaggerated accounts. The magazines were proudly displayed for visitors to see and admire and sometimes borrow.

Many times over the following years we invited John to pay another visit, but he always declined, saying that he was too old. Eventually his letters ceased and as I had now emigrated to England I wrote putting my English address on the back of the envelope. The letter was returned unopened and written across the front were the words, 'This person is now deceased.' We were not notified of his death by his son, nor did we ever learn the manner or date of his passing.

CHAPTER 25

AEROPLANE

I T WAS A beautiful summer's morning and as it was Sunday there were not many chores to be done. In dry weather water had to be drawn from the river in galvanized buckets to fill the barrels, which were used for storing water for daily domestic use, and that was the job allocated to my brother Tony and me that memorable morning in 1942. Half way through our chore we heard the drone of an aeroplane. This was not unusual in our part of the country as World War II was raging, and although we were a neutral country this did not prevent the planes from going astray and wandering into our airspace. Mayo was on the direct flight path for the American forces travelling to England. We regularly saw the Flying Fortresses thundering overhead and were glad we were at peace, although we suffered shortages and had rationing, but not so severe as our neighbour, England.

We waited for the plane to come into view from across the hills in great anticipation, but instead of it veering to the right and disappearing out over the Atlantic, it practically touched the mountain top, veered left and hovered over our common. We could plainly see the pilot and crew as the plane circled around as if looking for a safe landing spot. Everyone, young and old, were out of their houses wondering if war had come uninvited to our village. Animals were going berserk and the children were hoping that the pilot would land his aircraft on the common, but alas no such luck. He circled, gained height and turned back across the hills and brought his plane down in the bog about two miles away, practically on the banks of the River Moy, without injury to himself or crew. We were so disappointed. We found out afterwards that he intended ditching his plane but thought the common was a marsh and was scared of being swallowed up, not realising that Irish marshes are not as boggy as American ones.

I don't recall going to mass that Sunday morning, I only remember that within a few hours the roads and paths were dotted with people coming in all directions to view this monster that had landed in our midst and hoping to catch a glimpse of the foreigners also. The *Gardai* had been informed and had come in force to take those intruders into safe keeping. The appropriate authorities had to be notified in Northern Ireland. The crew were placed in temporary accommodation in the school house and given civilian clothes, as uniforms were not permitted to be worn in the Irish Free State by people engaged in war outside our country. A few days later they were duly escorted over the border. It was a nine-day wonder, and people from the borders of neighbouring counties came to gawk and talk and admire, while the families who owned the turf banks watched helplessly as their turf was trampled by myriads of feet.

A local man who had been in the bog when the plane came down jumped into a bog-hole and nearly drowned with fright as he was sure he was about to meet his maker. The neighbours said, 'Serve him right, working on a Sunday, profaning the Lord's Day,' when he had only come to get a bag of turf for the fire. Eventually the aircraft technicians came from Northern Ireland and dismantled the monster that had dropped out of the sky. It was the first manifestation of the war that raged outside our country and made us realize the horror of the consequences for the people involved. From then on the prayer for peace, which was said at the end of each mass throughout the land, was said with greater fervour in our own local church of St Joseph.

The locals who owned the turf banks demanded compensation before they allowed the dismantled plane to be loaded onto the transporters. The matter was settled amicably and within a few weeks our area was back to normal, but the event was the main topic of conversation for many months.

In 1944 another plane, this time a German one, came down

AEROPLANE

across the River Moy and nearer the sea. This happened of an afternoon, as people were working in the fields. They were terrified, as were the animals. There were pigs rooting nearby and they ran amok. In their panic they jumped stone ditches at heights that would do justice to a racehorse. Curiosity again brought people, especially the youngsters, to enjoy this spectacle and this time we were allowed inside to marvel at this German vehicle of war, that could unleash weapons and create havoc by the mere press of a button.

To us this was a memorable experience. For months afterwards the local wits entertained everyone with their varied stories of events surrounding this unusual occurrence in our peaceful countryside. They vied with each other as to who could tell the tallest tale. As to the fate of the pigs, some said that after scaling the ditches they headed for the river and dived in, and their breast stroke was something to be seen. Others likened it to the biblical story about the pigs being possessed, when they heard the plane crash they thought it was the last day and would not wait for judgment.

There were hosts of claims by local farmers for animals that were hurt in their flight, including a cow that was supposed to have landed in a tree. There were further claims for damage to property, but I don't recall those claims ever being resolved. One wit claimed to have seen a letter written by one of the crew to his mother while he was in temporary custody, 'Dear Ma, just to let you know I'm in County Mayo, Ireland. Our plane ran out of fuel, but we landed safely. You will never believe this, but the pigs here can fly and the cows climb trees. Hens, ducks and geese also roost in trees. Your loving son, Hans.' There was a rumour going round that in this case the grounding was deliberate, that the fuel was jettisoned because the crew were weary of fighting.

In the County of Roscommon, there was a similar occurrence but this time the plane was pilotless as the crew had baled out. They were Canadians and the plane caught fire as it hit the ground, but was only partially damaged. This happened while most people were in bed, but the local youngsters were coming from the dance hall. They saw the fire in the distance but did not pay much attention as they thought it was someone's hay stacks on fire. On the way to school the next morning, children found the damaged plane and took away some souvenirs. They found loose bullets and not being aware of their explosive content played with them. One boy threw a bullet on to the open turf fire in his home. When it exploded it went straight up the wide chimney, otherwise it could have had fatal consequences. The family said it was the best cleaning the chimney ever had!

CHAPTER 26

MATCH-MAKING
AND WATTLING

UGH DEMPSEY WAS fifty: a confirmed bachelor, or so the locals said. It was not that he did not want matrimony. He chased the girls, young and old, but none of the local lassies would go a-courting with him. They led him a merry dance though, promising him undying love and, by the way, fighting over his favours, but it was all part of a game to them. Hugh went to every dance and wake and anywhere there was a gathering of youngsters. The local lads would fix him up with some nice girl, unknown to her of course, and Hugh would set off on his bike washed and shaved, and sporting his best cap to cover his ever-receding hair line. He would wait for hours at some bridge or crossroads for his would-be sweetheart but of course she never turned up, and poor Hugh would go home dejected, telling every one he met that so-and-so let him down; but there must be good reason, for wasn't he a man of substance with a nice little farm, a new house, and not a bad-looking chap into the bargain? In fact the Good Lord had not endowed him with good looks or physique. He was tall and lean, walked with a stoop and looked much older than his fifty years. He was determined not to die a bachelor, so when all failed he had to resort to the old custom of match-making. He sent word to my father through an intermediary to start the proceedings. This was to be a new experience for my father, but an honour also, as he was considered the only person in the area suited to conduct this courteously and honourably.

The operation had to be worked out with military precision. Our village was agog with excitement at the prospect of Hugh at last acquiring a wife. Men from near and far came to our house at night, all giving advice and helping with good-natured banter. First of all, names of spinster ladies would be put forward and then rejected as we realized that Hugh himself would have probably approached these unwed maidens at some previous time. So after many nights of deliberation, and jubilation, it was decided that my father would have to direct his enquiries further afield. That meant that on the next big fair day – which was held in the nearest town on the twelfth of May – word would be passed around the pubs, eating houses and wherever there was an assembly where general conversation was in progress, that a man from a certain parish was looking for a spouse. As people came to this fair from all parts of the county it was generally anticipated that a suitable partner would be found for Hugh.

A certain pub in the town was named as the future rendezvous for all information to be collected and processed, and in due course names of the ladies interested in match-making were submitted by family and friends wishing to marry off someone. Meetings were arranged and information and details of both parties exchanged. It was a long process as the lady finally selected lived about thirty miles away and was unknown in our part of the county.

Before the couple met, members of her family had to come and inspect the land and house and would-be groom. That morning, our cattle had been driven into Hugh's field to enlarge his small herd. Nobody wrestled with their consciences over this bit of deceit as they believed that the ends would justify the means. Hugh's old mother was warned to be on her best behaviour and neighbours spring-cleaned the house. Everything was ready for inspection and the matchmaker and his advisers escorted the bride-to-be's people around the farm. Unknown to Hugh, he had been temporarily endowed with land by one of the party carried away by the Guinness and *poteen* that flowed freely on an occasion like this. The strangers were highly entertained so that, by the time of their departure, they had forgotten what they came for, and a favourable account was conveyed to Lena, his prospective bride.

It was now time to arrange a meeting between the couple and negotiate the dowry. This part of the proceedings was very important as money had to be handed over and signed for, to be banked until the marriage was contracted. A private room in a public house was granted free for the transaction, as business was mixed with pleasure, and a fair amount of alcohol was consumed. By now, the proprietor would be taking an active part as people in the pub would want information as to how things were progressing. Eventually all the preliminaries were completed, the wedding date set, and Hugh and Lena were joined in holy matrimony.

Invitations to the wedding party were by word of mouth. This was a night not to be missed. The older people were generally asked to an arranged wedding, but the youngsters also had their part to play as was the custom. It was called 'wattling'. The young, and not so young, would put on fancy dress, cover their faces, and make themselves as unrecognizable as possible. A leader would then be selected and about midnight they would converge on the house and demand entrance by rapping as loudly as possible on the door with a stick. The door had to be opened by the groom, who had to welcome them. A grand entrance would be made and drinks offered to all. Then the leader would demand that the new mistress of the house would honour the wattlers by dancing with him, and then the devilment would begin. Sometimes, for fun, they would pretend to

abduct the new lady of the house and hide her from the bride-
groom. Then the young women wattlers would fawn over the
newly wed man and pretend that they were broken-hearted
because he was no longer available. This went on for some time
until both sides tired.

The main function of the group was to make sure that the
happy couple fulfilled their marital obligations, so they duly saw
them to their bed-chamber with great pomp and ceremony. It
was not unknown for last-minute nerves, or shyness or fear, to
force one or the other of the newly-weds to flee from the house
on their wedding night. Hence the role of the wattlers was to
guard the windows and doors until morning to prevent escape.
Of course it was performed willingly and with good-natured
advice to the couple. In the meantime, the dancing and music
and merrymaking continued and a great night was enjoyed by
all.

Those of us too young to go to the party had to wait for
Sunday to see Lena at mass. We all gaped, and everyone had
their own comments. She was thin as a rake and of indetermi-
nate age. The oddest thing about her appearance was that she
used henna to colour her hair red. This was unheard of at the
time and caused much mirth and gossip. The women that
walked our way from mass were certain that she was past child-
bearing age, but that she would lighten the load of housework
for poor old Marie, Hugh's mother. No two people were ever

watched so closely as Lena and Hugh. Their every move was recorded and elaborated on. People could not believe that they could be so happy. Hugh was like a young man dancing attendance on his new wife, while she in turn, eventually presented him with a daughter.

By this time the locals had begun to grow fond of Lena as she had a warm personality and made herself at home amongst the neighbours. The birth of Maureen caused people to come once more to their door to offer sincere congratulations, and there was none so welcome as my own father who was the instigator of it all. Lena had always great affection for him, as he was the only person she knew when she started her new life among strangers.

By the time I grew up she was fully integrated into the community and I used to go visiting with my mother to her house in the next village. Hugh's mother, Marie, was able to take things easy in her old age. She was so happy with her grandchild and so thankful for her daughter-in-law. There was harmony in that household. Lena used to tell my mother that she was ever thankful of having a home of her own where she could sit at her own fireside with her family, as previously she had been living with her brother and his family and dreaded the thought of being beholden to others for her home as well as the pity of idle gossipers in her native village.

CHAPTER 27

THE WAKE

T HE POSTMAN WAS the purveyor of all news, good or bad; and as bad news travels fastest of all, Seamus's soul had not reached its maker before all the youngsters in the area had made plans to give him a good send off.

Traditionally, we all sat with the body in the house without any invitation from the family. It was supposed to be a prayerful vigil but in many cases, this was not so. It all depended on the deceased: if he or she were held in high esteem they received greater respect, but if the departed happened to be disliked by the majority, then the wake was a night to be enjoyed.

Old Seamus Rua ('Red Seamus') was not highly regarded. He was a prosperous bachelor who lived alone and was known for his ill-tempered nature. As this was to be my initiation into the grown-up world, at the age of fourteen, my enthusiasm knew no bounds. My daily chores were performed that evening with unusual haste and I donned my Sunday clothes, sneaked my sister's waving tongs and, not being well-versed in the art of hair-waving, scorched half my head.

I found a piece of red Christmas decoration paper, wet it and rubbed it into my cheeks. I must have looked like a clown but nevertheless, I was on my way, my heart bursting with joy at the prospect of being one of the grown-ups and of venturing into this secret society.

We all met at a pre-arranged meeting-place, Attymass Bridge, and headed in the direction of the wake-house, where we knelt and paid our homage to the corpse, laid out in his dark brown habit with his rosary entwined around his cold, yellow fingers. We murmured the usual to his next of kin about him looking grand and peaceful and offered the usual condolences, saying we knew he was in heaven as he was a good man. Duty done, we found seats at the end of the big kitchen. We told stories and jokes and were generally enjoying ourselves.

It was the custom in those days to give food to all comers, and we sat and watched people being taken to the parlour but, alas, no such invitation was extended to us. We had come miles and it would be daybreak before we could find our way home. This abuse of hospitality did not go unnoticed.

One of the more observant amongst us happened to notice that the corpse was roped down, as is the case when the spine

THE WAKE

curves. One of our more daring young men found a knife and cut the rope. The corpse sprung up straighter than he had been for many years and there were screams and a mass exodus from the house. Needless to say, we had to beat a hasty departure, but not without something to eat. Someone had taken advantage of the situation and filled their pockets. We divided the spoils and wound our way homeward without a care in the world.

Next morning the postman was at my mother's doorstep bright and early, with all the sordid details of the previous night's dastardly deeds and a bit more added on. He also informed my mother that three or four of her own family were involved, that we played havoc on our journey home, forgot to close gates when we used paths across fields and that different families from various villages on our route home were scouring the countryside trying to locate animals that had strayed through the open gates. He also told of how we had persuaded some poor young man who was not in full control of his wits to steal a soda-cake and a pot of jam, with the promise of fixing him up with a pretty young colleen who had no intention of going within courting distance of him, but who walloped him when he tried to claim his prize.

My poor mother was mortified listening to all this. Of course, we disappeared, but in due course hunger made us return to the fold, and my mother ranted and raved about the kind of family she was rearing, how she would never show her face in public again as she was so ashamed.

We all vigorously denied being directly involved in those misdeeds but all she would say was, 'Ye were part of the group, therefore ye must bear the responsibility also. And bear this in mind forever: Ye will be judged by the company ye keep. There's an old saying, "tell me who's your company and I'll tell you what you are."' 'If you could not honour the dead, how could you respect the living?' was another remark my mother made which still rings in my ears.

CHAPTER 28

THE O'FLYNNS

OUR PARISH OF Attymass was in its infancy, as our first church of St Joseph was not built until 1835. Our third pastor, Fr O'Flynn, arrived in our midst in 1845. He came from County Leitrim and was allocated a house and land about half a mile from the church. The house was situated just off the main road which at that time was only a dirt track or boreen. This boreen in turn bordered the lake, and in winter was flooded. It was to this house, known as the Cross House because of its shape, that our priest and his brother Tom came in those pre-famine years. He died in 1855 after witnessing the death and destitution of some of his parishioners through the Great Hunger of 1845–7.

His brother married and settled in Carrick and over a hundred years later, when I visited the same house, it was occupied by a very genteel family, the descendants of Fr O'Flynn's brother. They were all getting on in years. The female members, namely Lena, Kate and Murriah, were all spinsters and Thomassey, their brother, was also unmarried. The women dressed in the long, dark clothes fashionable in the previous century, with handmade lace attached to the blouses and bonnets. They were well off and lived comfortably. They were the only house in the parish, along with the priest and the teacher, to have servants. They were well educated and people respected them for their knowledge. Lena and Kate who were now retired, had been teachers in the local school.

Thomassey was six feet and nine inches tall, with a handlebar moustache. He used to wear a cravat and brown corduroy trousers and cap. His shoes were like boats, they must have been a size sixteen. His legs were as long as today and tomorrow, and as he walked his knees jerked forward. Watching him one imagined that he was about to collapse. He was greatly respected and considered a good farmer. He had one drawback, though: he would waylay any unattached female of advancing years, and not being well-versed in the art of courtship, his approach to the opposite sex and his crude chat-up lines were legendary.

He knew the healing potential of the plants and herbs that grew in abundance in our bogs and surroundings, and he was renowned for his gift of healing animals, giving his services freely. It was considered a privilege for him to visit and when he sent word to my mother that he was about to call, we would be warned to be on our best behaviour and to keep still, as when Thomassey sat down he would take up half the kitchen. He would sit by the table the far side of the room and his legs would reach the dresser on the other side. We could not resist the challenge of jumping back and forth across his legs, and there was enough space for three or four of us to play this game at the same time. My mother would be mortified, and after Thomassey's departure we would be walloped and reminded that our brothers depended on the O'Flynn family for employment.

They treated their employees with the greatest consideration and three of my brothers were indeed fortunate to have been in their employ for many years. For my brothers it was a continuation of their education, as after mealtimes there was a period of relaxation and a chance for the ex-teachers, Lena and Kate, to do their tutoring. Although my brothers may have been unwilling pupils at first, eventually they succumbed and acquired a knowledge and a love of books that was to last a lifetime. Thomassey also taught them good husbandry, and as the servant girl, Mary, was a good cook and as generous to my brothers as she was to her employers, my brothers were indeed lucky.

The visit to the little palace with its many rooms and corridors was the greatest treat in my young life, but there were two things that marred these visits. The O'Flynns owned the most ferocious dog in the neighbourhood. He was as big as a St Bernard and looked like a cross between a collie and a bear. My heart would be in my mouth as I ventured up the drive to deliver the missionary magazines that the family subscribed to. It was a great honour to be chosen for this task, and as there was always a treat in store for me, the fear of the mad dog would be overcome by the vision of the high tea which Mary would prepare for me on the instructions of her mistress.

There was also a beautiful flower garden with a white iron gate leading from the hall door, and I would be escorted to the hallowed ground to admire the profusion of flowers which Lena had cultivated as this was her domain. I would be given cuttings and seeds and instructed in the art of drying flowers. Sometimes I planted the seeds and cuttings in my own garden, but while I was at school our hens would invade my precious corner of the garden and would give themselves soil baths in my flower beds. I would cry and scold my mother, but was told hens were layers of eggs and flowers were only beholding to the eye.

The second thing that marred my visit was that the O'Flynn house had an unwanted guest – a ghost or spirit. I was always fearful of being left alone as I expected it to materialize and drag me into the space allocated to it, a portion of a room, measuring a few feet, which was boarded off and completely sealed without a doorway. The story told about the ghost was

that in the previous century, Fr O'Flynn was asked by a parish-
ioner to exorcise a spirit from his home. It proved too stubborn
for the priest but, pitying the family concerned, he demanded
that the spirit should come home with him where it would abide
until its earthly penance was fulfilled.

My visit over I would be accompanied by one or two of the
sisters and the dog Bran, who had now become friendly, to the
path by the lake which was to the east of the house. This path
followed a stream by the edge of the wood and was a short cut
home. Farewells would be said by the lake with warnings not to
wander off the path. I would go on my way carefree and happy,
thankful of having spent an evening in the company of the
sisters.

Among the many superstitions circulating in my home area
in my youth was that the banshee, a wailing fairy woman,
followed families whose name began with 'O' or 'Mc' and would
sometimes give these families ample warning of an impending
death. The person concerned did not have to live in the area,
they could be in any part of the world, but the banshee would
sing her last dirge around the home of whomsoever was depart-
ing this world. People would bless themselves and say, 'God
save us from harm,' and wonder which family this harbinger of
death was warning.

When I was about eleven years old, my sister and I had
been to great-aunt Ellen's some miles away from home. Before

we left Ellen would remind us not to dawdle and to get home while it was still light, warning us of the fairies and creatures who walked abroad in the darkness who were not of this world. Near our home was an ancient path which crossed the hills and followed the edge of the marsh. This road was sometimes traversed by a ghostly army, marching in single file with a burning flame held high to light their eerie way as they crossed the river and fields on to the fairy fort, where the light would disappear into the darkness. This phenomenon was witnessed many times during my early years and caused great consternation in our village. Some people believed that the fairy fort was really an ancient burial ground and that the marching army was a ghostly re-enactment of a burial procession across its old paths, while sceptics said that the lights were simply fluorescence from the bog. It was also said that the fairies were the remnants of a people known as the *Fir Bolg* or Belly Men, because they wore layers of leather around their bellies, who had invaded Ireland in pre-Christian times. The *Fir Bolg* were a short people who were eventually conquered by taller pagan invaders named the *Tuatha De Danaan*. Those *Fir Bolg* who were not killed went underground and survived by creeping out at night to steal from their conquerors. From this developed the folklore of a race of small people with supernatural powers.

My sister and I had to pass this point in the road, and we would quake with fear in case the soldiers of old would materialize and we would be lost forever. We had just crossed this great divide and were just in sight of our home with its welcoming light shining through the ever open door, when an unearthly cry rent the air, a most dismal, mournful sound filled with melancholy that pierced the heart. It seemed to come from far in the distance then, in a split second, it was beside us, reverberating around the hills, bringing the people of the village to their doors. Sound travels in a clear atmosphere and we could hear our own family but we could not call out. My sister took flight for the security of home, leaving me to the banshee. The desolate pain of fear gripped me, my heart stood still and I froze in horror and fell in a heap on the road. I was rescued by my mother and brother and I was in shock the whole night, but thankful to be in the land of the living. When another brother who worked for the O'Flynns came home later that night, he informed us that Kate was dying. We then knew that it was the banshee lamenting the departure of one of her kin.

On the demise of Lena and Thomassey, the wailing was heard again. Brought up on a daily diet of legends, myths and ghost stories, we were fascinated by the paranormal. Now, if any such ghosts or goblins should chance to wander around the same area, they will have to negotiate hundreds of acres of forest, as trees now grow where there was once nothing but marsh and bog, and the old paths and haunts are lost forever. The streams and rivers have dried to a trickle as the trees demand all the water. The village is practically dead, with only two families left.

The O'Flynns were Catholic, but it seems they were of Protestant stock. The word Protestant was never mentioned in our locality, and offspring of mixed marriages or converts were referred to as having the 'black drop in them'. Thomassey attended mass only once a year at Christmas, while the sisters always fulfilled their obligatory religious duties. They would drive in their pony and trap acknowledging the salutations of the less well-off, who had no means of transport and walked many miles in all types of weather to church.

Thomassey's services were required at Christmas when parishioners had to pay their Christmas dues, which were offerings for the upkeep of the priest and the parochial house. Thomassey was the only man who knew everyone in the parish, even using their correct names when most were only known by nicknames. He had a great bass voice and would stand by the church door calling out the names of the person entering and their respective village. At a table in the porch sat a representative of each village, who entered the amount given in a ledger. On the following Sunday, the amount donated by each household would be read out for all and sundry to hear, and of course this caused some embarrassment for the not so well-off members of the community. Eventually, as people became more enlightened, the custom was abolished. But I suppose it served its purpose, as people felt obliged to pay.

THE O'FLYNNS

If Thomassey wanted to emphasize a point, he would use some old phrases such as, 'Be the birth of my oath' – 'It's true what I'm telling ye.' If someone was passing his door while a churning was in progress, he was as superstitious as everyone else and they would be invited in to 'Strike a blow on the churn.' This was because people believed that while a churning was in process anyone entering a house or passing by had to lend a hand or the butter would be lost.

In 1942 there was a great storm and the roofs were blown off the O'Flynns' barns. During the reconstruction, a griddle was found in the rafters of the cow-byre. The news travelled fast, and many theories were put forward as to why a cooking utensil would be incorporated into the building of a cow-byre: it was to ward off the evil eye, or, as it was believed, it would stop fairies from stealing the milk if something used by human hands in the hearth of the house was built into a cow-byre. It was part of the mythology attached to cows and practised and believed by people in Ireland not so long ago.

I was presented with the griddle by Thomassey and Lena, and its age then was estimated to be over one hundred years. It was used to make potato bread for many years and then, with the dawning of a new era and loaf bread being readily available, the art of making potato bread was forgotten. So the griddle was assigned to an out-house and eventually disappeared. By this time I had emigrated and that piece of history faded from my memory until forty-five years afterwards, when visiting my old home again, I was presented with my old griddle by my brother Martin, who had unearthed it while trying to tame the wilderness which had once been a thriving vegetable garden of my home. It was a bit the worst for wear, but once again I am the proud possessor of a piece of history which I cherish, in memory of those wonderful people who were an integral part of our community.